SELECT

Betty Crocker's

DINNER FOR TWO

A BANTAM PREMIUM BOOK

BANTAM BOOKS
TORONTO · NEW YORK · LONDON · SYDNEY

This Bantam Premium book
features selected text from
Betty Crocker's Dinner for Two,
revised edition, published by
Golden Press, New York, 1980.

SELECTIONS FROM BETTY CROCKER'S DINNER FOR TWO

*A Bantam Premium Book / published by arrangement with
Western Publishing Company, Inc.*

PRINTING HISTORY

Bantam Premium edition / February 1982

Bantam Books are published by Bantam Books, Inc. Its trademark, consisting of the words "Bantam Books" and the por-
trayal of a rooster, is Registered in U.S. Patent and Trademark
Office and in other countries. Marca Registrada. Bantam
Books, Inc., 666 Fifth Avenue, New York, New York 10103.

PRINTED IN THE UNITED STATES OF AMERICA

CONTENTS

WHAT'S SO SPECIAL
ABOUT COOKING FOR TWO?

Two is a very good number. Or so the songwriters say. The joys of being a twosome have been catalogued in enough lyrics to reach the moon (in June) and back again. But somehow, very few of the choruses praise the pleasures of cooking for two.

Could it be because it's considered more of a problem than a pleasure? If so, this book will surely help dispel that notion. Not that the shopping, planning and prepartion involved are all fun and games. But there are some very definite advantages to setting two places (or even one) which you may not have given much thought to before.

Plotting the Plan

The twosome does have special problems, it's true. But chin up—this book will show you how to tackle them. To begin with, there's the matter of marketing. A major dither for anyone, but particularly so for doubles or singles. But all the recipes in this book are just the right size, so you'll know exactly how much to buy. You'll find solutions for other problem posers, too. There are complete meal plans for rush times, for tight-money times, for urge-to-splurge times. All just for two. But that doesn't mean you have to think small. The "Planning Ahead" chapter actually encourages you to think big—to take advantage of the economies and pleasures of family-size roasts and the variety that can come from their leftovers.

What's more, every single recipe and every menu has been tested in the Betty Crocker Kitchens and by twosomes all across the country. So we know they'll work for you.

Once you've tried these menus "by the book," feel free to improvise—to put new lyrics to the music. Switch vegetables, swap salads, ring in a different entrée. For a heartier meal, add rolls or biscuits; for a lighter one, ease up on dessert.

The Balancing Act

So you make your menu by putting your favorites together, right? Not quite. Good nutrition counts, too. And heavily. The menus in the book were planned with an eye to nutritional balance, so you're bound to pick up a tip or two. And you can do the same on your own by keeping the following guidelines in mind:

THE BASIC FOODS
You Need These Every Day

1. **Meats:** 2 or more servings (also includes poultry, fish, eggs, dried beans or peas and peanut butter)

2. **Vegetables and Fruits:** 4 or more servings (plan on one dark green or yellow vegetable every other day and one citrus fruit daily)

3. **Milk:** 2 or more cups (also includes cheese and ice cream)

4. **Breads and Cereals:** 4 or more servings (whole grain, enriched, restored or fortified)

Remember to include sweets, fats and extra servings from the basic food groups to help round out meals and provide additional food energy and food values.

WHEN MINUTES
MATTER

**Easy dinners that let you shortcut—
without being shortchanged**

**Steak Stroganoff
Parsleyed Noodles
Buttered Asparagus Spears
Herbed Tomatoes
Individual Brownie Alaskas**

*What does it say about you if dinner takes but 20
minutes from in-the-door to at-the-table? It says
that you're an advance planner, just waiting for
countdown. First, on with the water (for the
noodles and frozen asparagus), next to the stroganoff and finally the salad. The dessert's in the
freezer; the meringue top browns while instant
coffee brews.*

4

STEAK STROGANOFF

   1 **medium onion, thinly sliced**
   1 **tablespoon salad oil**
   2 **beef cubed steaks**
   2 **tablespoons flour**
   2 **tablespoons salad oil**
   ½ **teaspoon salt**
   ¼ **cup dairy sour cream**
   1 **can (2 ounces) mushroom stems and pieces**

In 8-inch skillet, cook and stir onion in 1 tablespoon oil until tender, about 4 minutes. Remove from skillet and set aside.

Coat steaks with flour. Heat 2 tablespoons oil in same skillet; cook steaks over medium heat, about 4 minutes on each side. Sprinkle with salt. Place steaks on warm platter or dinner plates.

Drain fat from skillet. Add onion, sour cream and mushrooms (with liquid) to skillet; heat, stirring occasionally. Serve sauce on steaks. *2 servings*.

PARSLEYED NOODLES

Cook 4 ounces noodles (about 1½ cups) in 1 quart boiling salted water (2 teaspoons salt) until tender, about 7 minutes. Drain noodles and return to saucepan. Add 1 tablespoon butter or margarine and 1 teaspoon parsley flakes and toss. *2 servings*.

HERBED TOMATOES

   1 **medium or 2 small tomatoes, cut into slices**
      Crisp salad greens
   2 **tablespoons oil-and-vinegar dressing**
      Salt and pepper
   ¼ **teaspoon freeze-dried chives**
      Dash thyme

Arrange tomato slices on salad greens. Drizzle dressing on tomatoes. Sprinkle with salt, pepper, chives and thyme. *2 servings*.

INDIVIDUAL BROWNIE ALASKAS

   2 **unfrosted brownies or date bars, 3x3 inches, or**
      commercially prepared sponge shortcakes
      Vanilla, coffee or peppermint ice cream
   1 **egg white**
   2 **tablespoons sugar**

Place brownies on ungreased baking sheet. Top each with scoop or slice of ice cream; place in freezer while preparing meringue. (Ice cream must be very hard before covering with meringue.)

   Heat oven to 450°. Beat egg white until foamy. Beat in sugar gradually; continue beating until stiff and glossy. Do not underbeat. Quickly spread meringue on ice cream *and sides of brownies*, being careful to seal meringue to baking sheet. Bake until light brown, about 3 minutes. Place in freezer (up to 24 hours) or serve immediately. *2 servings*.

**Quick Cheese Fondue
Crisp Green Salad
Fresh Fruit**

QUICK CHEESE FONDUE

- 1 can (11 ounces) condensed Cheddar cheese soup
- 1 cup shredded Cheddar, Swiss or Parmesan cheese (about 4 ounces)
- 2 green onions, finely chopped
- 1/8 teaspoon garlic powder
  Dash red pepper sauce
  Dippers (below)

In fondue pot, saucepan or chafing dish, heat soup and cheese over medium heat, stirring occasionally, until cheese is melted. Stir in onion, garlic powder and red pepper sauce. Serve with three or more of the Dippers, cut into bite-size pieces if necessary. If fondue becomes too thick, stir in small amount apple juice, white wine or beer. *2 servings*.

Dippers

Croutons
French bread
White or rye hard rolls
Toast sticks
Dried beef rolls
Cooked chicken or turkey
Frankfurters
Cooked ham
Luncheon meat
Cooked shrimp

Cooked asparagus
(crisp-tender)
Cooked broccoli (crisp-tender)
Cooked Brussels sprouts
(crisp-tender)
Cauliflower
Celery
Stuffed olives
Green onions
Green peppers
Cherry tomatoes

Liver Italiano
Spaghetti
Green Bean Tossed Salad
Lime Frappé
Vanilla Wafers

LIVER ITALIANO

2 tablespoons flour
½ teaspoon garlic salt
½ pound sliced beef liver, cut into 1-inch pieces
1 tablespoon salad oil
1 can (8 ounces) tomato sauce
1 green pepper, cut into thin strips
1 small onion, thinly sliced and separated into rings
3 to 4 ounces uncooked spaghetti
2 tablespoons grated Parmesan cheese

Mix flour and garlic salt; coat meat with flour mixture. Heat oil in 8-inch skillet; brown meat over medium heat. Stir in tomato sauce; add green pepper and onion. Cover and simmer until done, 8 to 10 minutes.

While meat simmers, cook spaghetti as directed on package. Serve meat mixture on spaghetti and sprinkle cheese on top. *2 servings*.

GREEN BEAN TOSSED SALAD

1 can (8 ounces) cut green beans, chilled
1 can (2 ounces) mushroom stems and pieces, chilled
1 cup bite-size pieces lettuce
1 teaspoon chopped pimiento
3 tablespoons Italian dressing
2 lettuce cups

Drain green beans and mushrooms. Toss beans, mushrooms, lettuce, pimiento and dressing in bowl. Divide salad between lettuce cups. *2 servings*.

LIME FRAPPÉ

2 cups crushed ice
½ can (6-ounce size) frozen limeade concentrate (about ¼ cup)*
2 tablespoons sugar
1 drop green food color

In blender, mix all ingredients on medium speed until mixture is consistency of sherbet. (Scrape sides once or twice if necessary.) Serve immediately or store in freezer until serving time. *2 servings*.

Note: To crush ice, use an ice crusher or wrap 9 or 10 ice cubes in towel and crush with mallet or hammer.

***Leftover limeade concentrate?** To the rescue for tomorrow's dessert: Top servings of cut-up fresh or canned fruit with spoonfuls of the partially thawed concentrate.

Smoked Pork Chops
Mashed Potatoes
Parsley-buttered Carrots
Sauerkraut Salad or Apple Slaw
Frosty Sherbet Sandwiches

SMOKED PORK CHOPS

Diagonally slash outer edge of fat on four ½-inch-thick smoked pork chops at 1-inch intervals to prevent curling. Set oven control at broil and/or 550°. Broil chops with tops 3 to 5 inches from heat until done, about 6 minutes on each side. *2 servings*.

Note: To panfry, rub 8-inch skillet with fat cut from chops. Cook chops over medium heat until done, about 3 minutes on each side.

PARSLEY-BUTTERED CARROTS

   1 **can (16 ounces) whole small carrots**
   1 **tablespoon butter or margarine**
   1 **teaspoon parsley flakes**

Heat carrots (with liquid); drain. Dot with butter. Sprinkle with parsley flakes and toss. *2 servings*.

Note: Use the vegetable cooking liquid in soups, gravies and sauces whenever possible, as it contains vitamins and minerals.

SAUERKRAUT SALAD

1 can (8 ounces) sauerkraut, rinsed and well drained
¼ cup chopped green pepper
1 tablespoon chopped red onion
1 tablespoon sugar
¼ teaspoon caraway seed
¼ teaspoon salt
  Dash pepper
2 tablespoons oil-and-vinegar dressing
  Crisp salad greens

Toss all ingredients except salad greens in bowl. Cover and refrigerate at least 30 minutes. Drain. Serve on salad greens. *2 servings*.

APPLE SLAW

1 pint coleslaw (from delicatessen)
1 red apple, chopped
  Crumbled blue cheese

Mix coleslaw and apple in bowl; garnish with cheese. *2 servings*.

FROSTY SHERBET SANDWICHES

1 can (8 ounces) sliced pineapple, drained
  Orange sherbet or vanilla ice cream
  Apricot preserves
  Diced roasted almonds

Place 1 pineapple slice on each dessert plate; top each with a scoop of sherbet. Cut 1 side of each remaining pineapple slice; twist and place on sherbet. Drizzle preserves on each serving; sprinkle with almonds. *2 servings*.

Herbed Lamb Chops
Quick au Gratin Potatoes
Broiled Zucchini
Broiled Tomatoes
Pears au Chocolat

HERBED LAMB CHOPS

   2 to 4 lamb rib, loin or shoulder chops, ¼ to 1 inch
       thick
   ¼ teaspoon oregano, rosemary or marjoram
       Salt and pepper

Set oven control at broil and/or 550°. Diagonally slash
outer edge of fat on chops at 1-inch intervals to prevent
curling. Sprinkle oregano on chops. Place chops on
rack in broiler pan. Broil with tops about 3 inches from
heat until brown, about 6 minutes on each side. Season
with salt and pepper. (Season after browning—salt
tends to draw moisture to surface and delays browning.) Garnish with mint jelly. *2 servings*.

QUICK AU GRATIN POTATOES

Measure contents of 1 package (5.5 ounces) au gratin
potatoes; divide in half (approximately 1 cup potato
slices and 3 tablespoons sauce mix).* Place half the
potato slices in 1-quart saucepan; sprinkle 3 tablespoons sauce mix on potato slices. Stir in half the
mounts of butter, water and milk called for on package. Heat to boiling, stirring occasionally. Reduce
heat; cover and simmer until potatoes are tender, about
20 minutes. *2 servings*.

*To store remaining mix, close package securely; use
within 2 weeks.

BROILED ZUCCHINI

Set oven control at broil and/or 550°. Remove stem and blossom ends from 2 medium zucchini. Cut each zucchini lengthwise in half.

Place cut sides down on rack in broiler pan. Broil about 3 inches from heat 6 minutes. Turn zucchini and brush each cut side with melted butter or margarine; season with salt and pepper. Broil until tender, about 6 minutes longer. *2 servings.*

BROILED TOMATOES

Set oven control at broil and/or 550°. Remove stem end from 1 medium tomato; cut tomato in half. Dot each half with ½ teaspoon butter or margarine; sprinkle with garlic salt, lemon pepper, and if desired, basil leaves, oregano leaves or savory. Broil tomato halves cut sides up with tops about 3 inches from heat until golden brown, about 5 minutes. *2 servings.*

PEARS AU CHOCOLAT

    1 can (8 ounces) pear halves, drained
    ⅛ teaspoon peppermint extract
    ½ can (17.5-ounce size) chocolate pudding (1 cup)

Place 2 pear halves in each dessert dish. Stir peppermint extract into pudding; spoon on pears. Garnish with dollop of whipped topping and maraschino cherry or mint leaf. *2 servings.*

Minute Steaks with Butter Sauce
Mashed Potatoes
Chili Mixed Vegetables
Stuffed Pear Salad
Cake Parfaits or Spanish Sundaes

MINUTE STEAKS WITH BUTTER SAUCE

  1 tablespoon salad oil
  2 beef cubed steaks
    Garlic salt
  2 tablespoons butter or margarine
  1 tablespoon lemon juice
  1 teaspoon Worcestershire sauce
  ½ teaspoon freeze-dried chives
  ¼ teaspoon dry mustard

Heat oil in 8-inch skillet; cook steaks over medium-high heat until brown, about 4 minutes on each side. Season with garlic salt. Remove steaks from skillet and keep warm.

Drain off fat. Melt butter in same skillet. Stir in remaining ingredients and heat. Place steaks on dinner plates; pour butter mixture on each. *2 servings*.

CHILI MIXED VEGETABLES

Cook ½ package (10-ounce size) frozen mixed vegetables as directed except—use only half the amounts of water and salt called for on package. Drain. Add 1 tablespoon butter or margarine and ¼ teaspoon chili powder and toss. *2 servings*.

STUFFED PEAR SALAD

Drain 1 can (8 ounces) pear halves. Arrange on crisp salad greens. Fill centers of pear halves with cranberry sauce or relish, raspberry or strawberry jelly, fruit-flavored gelatin cubes or peanut butter. *2 servings*.

CAKE PARFAITS

Cut pound cake (from freezer), leftover Quick Date Cake (page 96) or fig bars into cubes. Layer cubes alternately in parfait glasses with one of the following:

> Apricot or pineapple yogurt.
> Orange sherbet.
> Vanilla ice cream and chocolate sauce.
> Whipped topping and grated orange peel.

SPANISH SUNDAES

Divide ½ can (17.5-ounce size) vanilla pudding (1 cup) between dessert dishes. Drizzle chocolate syrup or sauce on each and top with Spanish peanuts. *2 servings*.

Chicken Livers with Mushrooms
Toast Points
Green Beans
Tomato-Grapefruit Salad
Butterscotch Cake Sundaes
or Nesselrode Sundaes

With this dinner plan, you can make it to the table in less than half an hour. Use frozen green beans, of course—perhaps with a crunchy sprinkling of almonds. The cake dessert's out of the freezer, too. Another day, another meal: the chicken livers on toasted English muffin halves or hot rice and the exotic Nesselrode dessert.

CHICKEN LIVERS WITH MUSHROOMS

½ pound fresh or frozen chicken livers
2 tablespoons butter or margarine
1 can (2 ounces) mushroom stems and pieces
¼ cup water
1 tablespoon flour
¼ teaspoon salt
⅛ teaspoon pepper
1 teaspoon parsley flakes
1 teaspoon instant chicken bouillon or 1 chicken
 bouillon cube
 Toast points

If using frozen chicken livers, thaw as directed on package or quick-thaw (see note at right). Cut livers into halves if necessary.

Melt butter in 8-inch skillet; brown livers over medium heat, stirring occasionally, 3 to 4 minutes. Stir in mushrooms (with liquid) and remaining ingredients except toast points. Heat to boiling. Reduce heat; simmer uncovered, stirring occasionally, until livers are done, about 5 minutes. Serve on toast points. *2 servings*.

Note: To quick-thaw livers, place them in melted butter in skillet. Cover and cook over medium heat until livers are thawed and can be easily separated, about 15 minutes. Remove cover; cook until livers are brown.

TOMATO-GRAPEFRUIT SALAD

  1 can (8 ounces) grapefruit sections, drained
  1 tomato, cut into wedges
     Salad greens
     Green pepper strips
     Clear sweet-and-sour dressing

Arrange grapefruit sections and tomato wedges on salad greens. Top salads with green pepper strips and drizzle with dressing. *2 servings*.

Variation

Tomato-Pineapple Salad: Substitute 2 pineapple slices for the grapefruit sections and cut tomato into slices.

BUTTERSCOTCH CAKE SUNDAES

2 slices pound cake (from freezer) or leftover
Gingerbread (page 49) or 2 commercially
prepared sponge shortcakes
Vanilla ice cream
Butterscotch ice-cream topping

Place cake slices on dessert plates; top with scoops of ice cream. Drizzle ice-cream topping on each. *2 servings*.

NESSELRODE SUNDAES

Heat ¼ cup Nesselrode mixture,* stirring occasionally. Soak 2 sugar cubes in orange extract 2 to 3 minutes. Place scoop of vanilla ice cream in each dessert dish. Spoon hot Nesselrode mixture on ice cream. Place a sugar cube on top of each sundae and ignite. *2 servings*.

*Extra Nesselrode? Use as a topping for vanilla, rice or tapioca pudding, lemon sherbet, pound cake or gingerbread. Or make Nesselrode Ice Cream (page 109).

London Broil
Mushroom Rice
Crisp Green Salad
Fresh Fruit and Cheese

LONDON BROIL

Score 1-pound flank steak; place in shallow glass dish. Pour ½ cup Italian dressing on steak. Cover and refrigerate at least 8 hours, turning meat occasionally.

Remove steak; reserve dressing. Set oven control at broil and/or 550°. Broil steak with top 3 to 4 inches from heat until medium rare, about 4 minutes on each side, brushing with reserved dressing several times. Cut meat across grain at a slanted angle into thin slices. *2 generous servings.*

MUSHROOM RICE

   Uncooked instant rice (enough for 2 servings)
1 teaspoon butter or margarine
1 can (2 ounces) mushroom stems and pieces, drained
¼ teaspoon parsley flakes

Cook rice as directed on package. Stir in butter, mushrooms and parsley flakes; heat through, stirring occasionally. *2 servings.*

FRESH FRUIT AND CHEESE

Serve a variety of fresh fruit and dessert cheeses (Gourmandise, Port du Salut, Swiss, Bel Paese, Cheddar, Gruyère, Edam, Gouda) on tray with dessert plates and small knives. Cheeses should be at room temperature.

**Broiled Ham and Sweet Potatoes
Brussels Sprouts with Cashews
Lettuce Wedges with Tangy Corn Dressing
Banana Fondue Fritters**

BROILED HAM AND SWEET POTATOES

    1 fully cooked smoked ham slice, about ½ inch thick
    1 can (8 ounces) sweet potatoes in syrup, drained
    2 canned pineapple slices, well drained*
    2 tablespoons orange marmalade

Set oven control at broil and/or 550°. Diagonally slash
outer edge of fat on ham slice at 1-inch intervals to
prevent curling. Place ham slice on rack in broiler pan.
Broil ham slice with top 3 inches from heat until light
brown, about 5 minutes.

Turn ham; place potatoes and pineapple on rack.
Brush marmalade on potatoes and pineapple. Broil
until potatoes and pineapple are hot and ham is light
brown, about 5 minutes. *2 servings*.

*Extra pineapple slices? Top with cottage cheese for
a salad.

BRUSSELS SPROUTS WITH CASHEWS

Cook 1 package (10 ounces) frozen Brussels sprouts as
directed. Drain and return to saucepan. Add 2 tablespoons cashews, walnuts or sliced water chestnuts and
1 tablespoon butter or margarine; heat through.
2 servings.

LETTUCE WEDGES WITH TANGY CORN DRESSING

Mix 2 tablespoons oil-and-vinegar dressing and ¼ cup corn relish.* Spoon on lettuce wedges. *2 servings*.

*Extra corn relish? Serve later in the week as a zesty accompaniment for roast pork, veal, ham or chicken.

BANANA FONDUE FRITTERS

    1 cup buttermilk baking mix
    ½ cup water
    1 egg
    ¼ teaspoon almond extract
      Salad oil
    2 bananas, cut into 2-inch slices
      Confectioners' sugar

Beat baking mix, water, egg and extract with rotary beater until smooth.

Pour oil into metal fondue pot to depth of 1 to 1½ inches. Heat on fondue stand over burner or on range to 375° or until 1-inch bread cube browns in 1 minute.

With long-handled fork, each person dips banana slice into batter, cooks it in hot oil until puffed and golden brown, then rolls fritter in confectioners' sugar. *2 generous servings*.

Variations

Apple Fondue Fritters: Substitute 2 apples, pared and cut into ½-inch slices, for the bananas. Roll fritters in cinnamon-sugar mixture instead of in confectioners' sugar.

Strawberry Fondue Fritters: Substitute ½ pint fresh strawberries for the bananas.

Tacos
Refried Beans
Fruit with Quick Custard Sauce

TACOS

½ pound ground beef
 1 can (8 ounces) tomato sauce
 2 tablespoons instant minced onion
½ teaspoon garlic salt
¼ teaspoon chili powder
    Dash pepper
 4 or 5 taco shells
½ to ¾ cup shredded lettuce
½ cup shredded natural Cheddar cheese
½ cup chopped tomato (if desired)
    Hot sauce (below) or bottled taco sauce

In 8-inch skillet, cook and stir meat until brown. Drain off fat. Stir in tomato sauce, onion, garlic salt, chili powder and pepper. Simmer uncovered 15 minutes.

While meat mixture simmers, heat taco shells as directed on package. Fill taco shells with meat mixture. Top each with lettuce, cheese and chopped tomato. Serve with Hot Sauce. *4 or 5 tacos.*

Hot Sauce
Mix ⅓ cup chili sauce and ¼ teaspoon red pepper sauce or 1 teaspoon minced hot chili pepper.

Note: Shredded Swiss or mozzarella cheese can be substituted for the Cheddar cheese. And for variety, when filling the taco shells, add one of the following: ¼ cup chopped avocado, ¼ cup chopped olives, ¼ cup chopped onion or ¼ cup chopped green pepper.

FRUIT WITH QUICK CUSTARD SAUCE

> 1 orange, pared and sectioned, or 1 can (11 ounces)
>   mandarin orange segments, drained
> 1 banana
> ¼ cup canned vanilla pudding
> 2 tablespoons milk

Divide orange sections between dessert dishes. Slice banana into dishes. Mix pudding and milk; spoon onto fruits. *2 servings*.

Variations

Pineapple with Quick Custard Sauce: Substitute 1 can (13½ ounces) pineapple chunks, drained and chilled, for the orange and banana. Top each serving with ½ teaspoon strawberry jelly.

Berries with Quick Custard Sauce: Substitute 1 cup strawberry halves, raspberries or blueberries for the orange and banana.

SOMETHING TO KNOW ABOUT . . .

Cut off the peel and white membrane of the orange. Then cut along both sides of each dividing membrane until you reach the core and can lift out the orange section.

Oven-fried Pike
Lemon-Chive Potatoes
Buttered Green Beans
Cabbage-Green Pepper Slaw
Peaches 'n Custard
or Spiced Fruit Compote

OVEN-FRIED PIKE

    1   pound fresh or frozen pike fillets
    2   tablespoons butter or margarine
    ½   teaspoon salt
    ¼   teaspoon pepper
    ¼   cup all-purpose flour or buttermilk baking mix
        Paprika
        Tomato wedges
        Lemon wedges

Heat oven to 500°. If using frozen fillets, thaw as directed on package. In oven, melt butter in shallow baking dish. Sprinkle salt and pepper on fish, then coat with flour and place in baking dish. Sprinkle paprika on fish. Bake uncovered until fish flakes easily with fork, 10 to 15 minutes. Garnish with tomato and lemon wedges. *2 servings*.

LEMON-CHIVE POTATOES

    1   can (about 16 ounces) whole potatoes
    1   tablespoon butter or margarine
    2   teaspoons lemon juice
    ½   teaspoon freeze-dried chives.

Heat oven to 500°. Drain and rinse potatoes; place in ungreased 1-quart casserole. Cover potatoes with water. Cover and bake until potatoes are hot, 10 to 15 minutes. Drain. Add remaining ingredients and toss until potatoes are coated. *2 servings*.

CABBAGE-GREEN PEPPER SLAW

   ⅛ **medium green cabbage, cut into pieces**
   ½ **small green pepper, cut into pieces**
   2 **green onions, cut into pieces**
   ½ **teaspoon salt**
   2 **tablespoons coleslaw dressing**

Place cabbage, green pepper and onions in blender; cover with cold water. Chop 3 to 5 seconds. Drain thoroughly in colander or sieve. Mix vegetables, salt and dressing. *2 servings*.

PEACHES 'N CUSTARD

   ½ **cup canned vanilla pudding**
   2 **teaspoons orange juice**
   1 **can (8 ounces) sliced peaches, drained**
   1 **teaspoon currant jelly**

Mix pudding and orange juice; chill. Divide peach slices between dessert dishes. Spoon pudding mixture onto peaches and top each serving with ½ teaspoon jelly. *2 servings*.

SPICED FRUIT COMPOTE

   1 **can (8 ounces) fruit cocktail or fruits for salad**
   ⅛ **teaspoon allspice**

Heat fruit cocktail (with syrup) and allspice to boiling. Serve warm. *2 servings*.

Hot Tomato Bouillon
Seafood Salad Bowl
Cheese-Onion Twists
Orange Slush
Chocolate Wafers

HOT TOMATO BOUILLON

¾ cup tomato juice
¼ cup water
1 beef bouillon cube

Heat all ingredients over medium-high heat to boiling,
stirring occasionally. Serve hot. *2 servings.*

SEAFOOD SALAD BOWL

1 can (4½ ounces) large shrimp, rinsed and drained
1 can (7½ ounces) crabmeat, drained and cartilage
   removed
6 cups bite-size pieces lettuce (iceberg, Bibb,
   romaine, leaf)
½ jar (6-ounce size) marinated artichoke hearts,
   drained
¼ cup sliced pitted ripe olives
1 hard-cooked egg, cut into wedges
½ teaspoon capers, if desired
   Freshly ground black pepper
   Italian dressing or creamy French dressing

Reserve some shrimp and crabmeat pieces for garnish.
Toss remaining shrimp, crabmeat, the lettuce, artichoke hearts and olives. Divide between salad bowls.

Garnish with reserved shrimp and crabmeat pieces, the egg wedges, capers and pepper. Serve with dressing. *2 generous servings*.

CHEESE-ONION TWISTS

   2 teaspoons instant minced onion
   1 tablespoon butter or margarine, softened
  ½ cup buttermilk baking mix
   2 tablespoons shredded Cheddar cheese
   2 tablespoons water
    Soft butter or margarine
    Caraway seed, dill weed or poppy seed

Heat oven to 425°. Mix onion and 1 tablespoon butter. Stir baking mix, cheese and water with fork to soft dough. Turn onto lightly floured cloth-covered board; smooth dough into ball and knead about 5 times. Pat or roll into rectangle, 8x6 inches.

Spread onion mixture on rectangle to within 2 inches of one long side. Beginning with plain side, fold lengthwise into thirds; press together. Cut crosswise into 6 strips. Twist each strip twice.

Place twists on ungreased baking sheet; press ends on sheet to fasten securely. Brush soft butter on twists; sprinkle with caraway seed. Bake until light brown, about 10 minutes. Serve warm. *6 twists*.

ORANGE SLUSH

In blender or small mixer bowl, mix 1 pint vanilla ice cream, softened, and ¼ cup frozen orange juice concentrate (thawed) until thick and smooth. Garnish each drink with orange slice and mint leaves. Serve with straws. *2 servings*.

Broiled Lamb Patties
Broiled Eggplant with Tomato Sauce
Wilted French Onion Salad
Warm Apricot Crunch Sundaes

BROILED LAMB PATTIES

> 2 lamb patties (4 ounces each)
> Salt
> Lemon pepper

Set oven control at broil and/or 550°. Place patties on rack in broiler pan. Broil with tops 3 to 5 inches from heat until brown, about 7 minutes. Sprinkle with salt and lemon pepper. Turn patties; broil until medium done, about 7 minutes. *2 servings*.

BROILED EGGPLANT WITH TOMATO SAUCE

> 1 small eggplant (about 1 pound), pared and cut into
>   ½-inch slices
>   Soft butter or margarine
>   Salt and pepper
> 1 can (8 ounces) tomato sauce
> ¼ teaspoon garlic powder

Set oven control at broil and/or 550°. Place eggplant slices on rack in broiler pan. Brush butter on slices; season with salt and pepper. Broil tops about 3 inches from heat until eggplant is hot and tender, about 6 minutes.

In small saucepan, heat tomato sauce and garlic powder, stirring occasionally. Serve on eggplant slices. *2 servings*.

WILTED FRENCH ONION SALAD

 1 small onion, thinly sliced and separated into rings
 2 to 4 cups bite-size pieces romaine
 ¼ cup oil-and-vinegar dressing
 2 teaspoons sugar
 ½ teaspoon instant beef bouillon
    Dash red pepper sauce
    Grated Parmesan or Swiss cheese
    Seasoned croutons

Toss onion rings and romaine in salad bowls. In small saucepan, heat dressing, sugar, bouillon and red pepper sauce to boiling, stirring occasionally. Drizzle hot dressing on salads; sprinkle with cheese and croutons. *2 servings.*

WARM APRICOT CRUNCH SUNDAES

 1 can (8 ounces) apricot halves, drained
 2 tablespoons brown sugar
 ¼ cup cashew halves
 1 tablespoon soft butter or margarine
    Vanilla ice cream

Set oven control at broil and/or 550°. Place apricots in 8-inch ovenproof skillet or shallow baking dish. Sprinkle sugar and cashews on apricots; dot with butter. Broil with tops about 6 inches from heat until sugar and butter are melted and sauce is bubbly, about 2 minutes. Serve immediately on ice cream. *2 servings.*

MORE DIMES
THAN DOLLARS

Inventive dinners that make the most
of a little money

Pork Chops Creole
Buttered Green Beans
Peanut Crunch Slaw
Cloverleaf Rolls
Mocha Parfaits

PORK CHOPS CREOLE

- 4 pork loin or rib chops, ½ to ¾ inch thick
- 1 teaspoon salt
- ¼ teaspoon pepper
- 4 thin onion slices
- 4 green pepper rings
- 4 tablespoons uncooked instant rice
- 1 can (8 ounces) stewed tomatoes

In 10-inch skillet, brown chops over medium heat. Sprinkle salt and pepper on chops. Top each with 1 onion slice, 1 green pepper ring, 1 tablespoon rice and ¼ cup tomatoes. Reduce heat; cover and simmer until done, about 45 minutes. (Add small amount of water if necessary). *2 servings.*

PEANUT CRUNCH SLAW

    2 tablespoons mayonnaise
    2 tablespoons dairy sour cream
    ½ teaspoon salt
    2 tablespoons chopped green onion
    2 tablespoons chopped green pepper
    ¼ cup chopped cucumber
    1 cup shredded cabbage
    ¼ cup thinly sliced celery
    2 tablespoons chopped salted peanuts
       Grated Parmesan cheese

Mix mayonnaise, sour cream, salt, onion, green pepper and cucumber in bowl. Stir in cabbage and celery. Sprinkle peanuts and cheese on each serving. *2 servings*.

MOCHA PARFAITS

    ¼ cup chilled whipping cream or ½ cup frozen
       whipped topping (thawed)
    2 teaspoons sugar
    ½ teaspoon powdered instant coffee
    ½ can (17.5-ounce size) chocolate pudding (1 cup)

In chilled bowl, beat whipping cream, sugar and instant coffee until stiff. (If using whipped topping, omit sugar and mix in instant coffee.) Alternate layers of pudding and whipped cream in parfait glasses or dessert dishes. Chill. Garnish with chocolate shot or chocolate curls. *2 servings*.

Mustard Short Ribs
Baked Sweet Potatoes
Italian Green Beans
Apple-Celery Toss or Cabbage Slaw
Butterscotch Bread Pudding

It's a toss-up . . . whether you'll want to liven this easy oven meal with the crisp and crunchy Apple-Celery Toss or the Cabbage Slaw. If time is of the essence, you might note that the slaw can be made ahead and refrigerated.

MUSTARD SHORT RIBS

  2 **pounds beef short ribs, cut into pieces**
  2 **medium onions, sliced**
  2 **tablespoons prepared mustard**
  1 **tablespoon lemon juice**
  1 **teaspoon sugar**
  1 **teaspoon salt**
 ½ **teaspoon instant minced garlic**
 ½ **teaspoon pepper**

Heat oven to 350°. In 8-inch skillet, brown meat over medium heat. Place meat and onion slices in ungreased 2-quart casserole. Mix remaining ingredients; pour on meat. Cover tightly and bake until meat is tender, about 1½ hours. *2 servings.*

BAKED SWEET POTATOES

Heat oven to 350°. Rub 2 medium sweet potatoes with shortening (for soft skins). Prick with fork to allow steam to escape. Bake until tender, about 1 hour.

To serve, cut crisscross gash in each top; squeeze gently until some of potato pops up through opening. Serve with butter or dairy sour cream. *2 servings*.

APPLE-CELERY TOSS

1½ **cups bite-size pieces lettuce**
  1 **red apple, sliced**
  ¼ **cup diagonally sliced celery**
  ¼ **cup mayonnaise or oil-and-vinegar dressing**

Combine lettuce, apple slices and celery in bowl. Pour mayonnaise on and toss. *2 servings*.

CABBAGE SLAW

  2 **cups coarsely shredded cabbage (about ⅓ head)**
  ¼ **cup coarsely chopped unpared cucumber**
     Dash salt
  ¼ **cup mayonnaise or salad dressing**

Combine cabbage, cucumber and salt in bowl. Pour mayonnaise on cabbage mixture and toss. *2 servings*.

BUTTERSCOTCH BREAD PUDDING

    1 cup soft bread cubes
    1 egg
    1 tablespoon butter or margarine, melted
    ⅔ cup milk
    3 tablespoons brown sugar
    ½ teaspoon cinnamon
    ¼ teaspoon nutmeg
       Dash salt
    ⅓ cup raisins

Heat oven to 350°. Place bread cubes in buttered 2½-cup casserole. Beat egg slightly; stir in butter, milk, brown sugar, seasonings and raisins. Pour egg mixture on bread cubes. Bake until knife inserted halfway between center and edge comes out clean, about 40 minutes. Serve warm. Top with light cream if you like. *2 servings*.

Eggs Delmonico
Nutmeg Spinach
Apple-Orange Pinwheel Salad
Coffee Crunch Bars

EGGS DELMONICO

 1 can (10½ ounces) condensed cream of mushroom
    or cream of chicken soup
 ½ cup shredded natural Cheddar cheese
 3 or 4 hard-cooked eggs, sliced
 1 tablespoon finely chopped pimiento
    Hot buttered toast or toasted English muffins
    Paprika or snipped parsley

In 1-quart saucepan, heat soup over medium heat until
hot and bubbly, 3 to 5 minutes. Stir in cheese; cook
over low heat, stirring occasionally, until cheese is
melted. Fold in eggs and pimiento; heat through, about
2 minutes. Serve on toast; sprinkle paprika on top. *2
servings*.

Variation

Creamed Eggs with Tuna: Use only 2 eggs and fold
in 1 can (3¼ ounces) tuna, drained and flaked.

NUTMEG SPINACH

  1 pound fresh spinach
  ½ teaspoon salt
  ⅛ teaspoon nutmeg
    Dash lemon pepper
  1 tablespoon butter or margarine

Remove imperfect leaves and root ends of spinach. Wash spinach; drain and place in large saucepan with just the water which clings to leaves. Cover and cook until spinach is wilted, 3 to 5 minutes. Drain. Stir in salt, nutmeg, lemon pepper and butter. *2 servings*.

Time-saver: Cook 1 package (10 ounces) frozen chopped spinach as directed; drain and season with nutmeg, lemon pepper and butter.

APPLE-ORANGE PINWHEEL SALAD

  1 red apple
  1 orange, pared and sectioned
    Crisp salad greens
    Honey Dressing (below)

Cut unpared apple into wedges. Arrange apple wedges and orange sections in pinwheel design on salad greens. Drizzle Honey Dressing on fruit. *2 servings*.

Honey Dressing

Mix ¼ cup mayonnaise or salad dressing, 2 tablespoons honey and 1½ teaspoons lemon juice.

COFFEE CRUNCH BARS

    1 cup all-purpose flour*
    ½ cup brown sugar (packed)
    ½ cup butter or margarine, softened
    2 to 3 teaspoons powdered instant coffee
    ¼ teaspoon baking powder
    ⅛ teaspoon salt
    ½ teaspoon vanilla
    ¼ cup chopped walnuts
    ½ cup semisweet chocolate pieces

Heat oven to 350°. Mix flour, sugar, butter, coffee, baking powder, salt and vanilla. Stir in nuts and chocolate pieces. Press mixture evenly into ungreased baking pan, 9x9x2 inches. Bake until light brown and crisp, 20 to 25 minutes. Cut into bars, 3x1½ inches, while warm. *18 bars*.

*If using self-rising flour, omit baking powder and salt.

Italian Spaghetti
Tossed Spinach Salad
Butter Sticks
Biscuit Tortoni

Honestly, now, would you peg this meal as a penny-squeezer? Double it when you have another twosome over and see if they don't say "Magnifico!" One reason: You cared enough to make those butter sticks from "scratch." And there's that special salad, too. As for dessert, it's one of the more costly ones when you order it in an Italian restaurant. Yet it takes so little time (and money) to make it at home this easy way.

ITALIAN SPAGHETTI

½ pound ground beef
3 tablespoons minced onion
1 can (8 ounces) tomato sauce
1 can (6 ounces) tomato paste
1 cup water
¼ teaspoon salt
¼ teaspoon garlic powder
¼ teaspoon oregano leaves
¼ teaspoon basil
3½ to 4 ounces uncooked spaghetti
   Grated Parmesan cheese

In 8-inch skillet, cook and stir meat until brown. Stir in remaining ingredients except spaghetti and cheese. Heat to boiling. Reduce heat; cover and simmer 1 hour. While sauce simmers, cook spaghetti as directed on package. Serve sauce on hot spaghetti; pass Parmesan cheese. *2 servings*.

TOSSED SPINACH SALAD

  2 **cups bite-size pieces spinach leaves (about 5 ounces)**
  2 **or 3 radishes, sliced**
  2 **slices onion, separated into rings**
     Oil-and-vinegar dressing

Toss spinach, radish slices and onion rings in bowl. Serve salad with oil-and-vinegar dressing. *2 servings*.

BUTTER STICKS

  ¼ **cup butter or margarine**
  1 **cup buttermilk baking mix**
  ¼ **cup water**
     Salt

Heat oven to 425°. In oven, melt butter in baking pan, 9x9x2 inches. Stir baking mix and water with fork to a soft dough. Turn onto floured cloth-covered board; smooth dough into ball and knead 5 times. Roll into rectangle, 6x4 inches. Cut into 8 strips, 4x¾ inch.

Dip each strip into melted butter, coating all sides, and arrange in pan. Sprinkle salt lightly on strips. Bake until golden brown, 10 to 12 minutes. *8 sticks*.

BISCUIT TORTONI

- **2 tablespoons vanilla wafer or macaroon crumbs**
- **1 tablespoon diced candied or well-drained maraschino cherries**
- **2 tablespoons diced roasted almonds**
- **½ pint vanilla ice cream (1 cup)**

Line 2 muffin cups with paper baking cups. Mix crumbs, cherries and almonds. Soften ice cream slightly; fold in crumb mixture. Divide ice-cream mixture between muffin cups. Decorate each with red cherry half and slices of green cherry to resemble a flower. Freeze until firm. *2 servings*.

**Crusty Curried Chicken with Biscuits
Buttered Broccoli
Green Bean-Tomato Vinaigrette
Frosted Melon Wedges with Berries**

CRUSTY CURRIED CHICKEN WITH BISCUITS

    2 tablespoons salad oil
    ½ cup buttermilk baking mix
    1 tablespoon curry powder
    1 teaspoon salt
    ⅛ teaspoon pepper
 1½ pounds chicken pieces or 2-pound broiler-fryer
        chicken, quartered
    1 cup buttermilk baking mix
    ¼ cup water
    2 canned peach halves, if desired

Heat oven to 425°. Pour oil into baking pan, 9x9x2 or
11¾x7½x1½ inches. Mix ½ cup baking mix, the
curry powder, salt and pepper; coat chicken with mixture. Place chicken skin side down in pan. Bake uncovered 35 minutes.

Mix 1 cup baking mix and the water to a soft dough.
Turn chicken, pushing pieces to one side of pan. Drop
dough by spoonfuls (5) into pan in single layer next to
chicken. Arrange peaches on chicken. Bake until biscuits are light brown and chicken is tender, about 15
minutes. *2 servings*.

Variation

Herbed Chicken with Biscuits: Substitute ¼ teaspoon thyme leaves and ¼ teaspoon rosemary leaves
for the curry powder.

BUTTERED BROCCOLI

Trim off large leaves of ¾ to 1 pound broccoli; remove tough ends of lower stems. Wash broccoli. If stems are thicker than 1 inch in diameter, make lengthwise gashes in each stem.

Heat 1 inch salted water (½ teaspoon salt to 1 cup water) to boiling. Add broccoli; cover and heat to boiling. Cook until stems are tender, 12 to 15 minutes. Drain; dot with 1 tablespoon butter or margarine. *2 servings*.

GREEN BEAN-TOMATO VINAIGRETTE

    1 can (8 ounces) cut green beans, drained
    ¼ pint cherry tomatoes, cut into halves
    1 small onion, sliced
    1 can (2 ounces) sliced mushrooms, drained
    ¼ cup Italian dressing

Toss all ingredients together in bowl. Cover and chill at least 2 hours, tossing occasionally. *2 servings*.

FROSTED MELON WEDGES WITH BERRIES

Place scoop of your favorite sherbet in center of each of 2 melon wedges; top each with ¼ cup berries. Here are some combinations you might like:

Honeydew melon, lemon or pineapple sherbet, raspberries or strawberries.

Cantaloupe or Persian melon, orange sherbet, blackberries.

Crenshaw melon, lime sherbet, blueberries or blackberries. *2 servings*.

Pot Roast with Carrots and Onions
Herbed Noodles
Tossed Green Salad
Whole Wheat Rolls
Warm Caramel Pears

POT ROAST WITH CARROTS AND ONIONS

2 tablespoons salad oil
2- pound beef chuck pot roast
½ teaspoon salt
¼ teaspoon pepper
½ cup water
4 medium carrots, halved lengthwise
4 small onions
¼ teaspoon salt
   Kettle Gravy (on page 44), if desired

Heat oil in Dutch oven or large skillet; brown meat over medium heat, about 15 minutes. Sprinkle ½ teaspoon salt and the pepper on meat. Add water; cover tightly and simmer on range or in 325° oven 1½ hours. (Add small amount of water if necessary.) Add vegetables and ¼ teaspoon salt; cook until meat is tender and vegetables are done, about ½ hour.

Place meat and vegetables on warm platter; keep warm while making gravy. Serve meat with gravy. *2 servings.*

KETTLE GRAVY

Skim excess fat from meat broth. Measure broth; if necessary add enough water (or vegetable cooking liquid, consommé or vegetable juice) to measure ½ cup and pour into pan. Mix 2 tablespoons cold water and 1 tablespoon flour. Stir flour mixture into broth. Heat to boiling, stirring constantly. Boil and stir 1 minute. If desired, stir in few drops bottled brown bouquet sauce. Season with salt and pepper. If you prefer a thinner gravy, stir in small amount of additional liquid. *½ cup*.

Note: If using quick-mixing flour, just stir into cold water with fork. If using regular flour, shake water and flour in covered jar—be sure to put water in jar first, then the flour.

SOMETHING TO KNOW ABOUT . . .

To insure that Kettle Gravy will be smooth, stir constantly as you add the flour-water to the broth. The broth will have more flavor and color if the meat was browned slowly.

HERBED NOODLES

      3 to 4 ounces uncooked noodles (1 to 1½ cups)
     ¼ teaspoon thyme leaves
     ¼ teaspoon basil leaves
     ¼ teaspoon snipped parsley
     ¼ teaspoon snipped chives or finely chopped onion
      1 tablespoon butter or margarine, melted

Cook noodles in 1 quart boiling salted water (1½ teaspoons salt) until tender, 7 to 10 minutes. Drain noodles and return to saucepan. Mix remaining ingredients; pour onto noodles and toss. *2 servings*.

WARM CARAMEL PEARS

      1 can (8 ounces) pear halves
         Vanilla ice cream
     ¼ teaspoon cinnamon
     ¼ cup caramel ice-cream topping

Heat pears (with syrup) in small saucepan. Drain. Spoon pears into serving dishes. Top with scoops of ice cream. Stir cinnamon into caramel topping. Pour on each serving. *2 servings*.

Barleyburger Stew
Hot French Bread
Fresh Vegetable Relishes (page 71)
Velvet Crumb Cake with Pineapple Sauce

BARLEYBURGER STEW

- ½ **pound ground beef**
- ½ **cup chopped onion**
- ¼ **cup chopped celery**
- 1 **can (18 ounces) tomato juice (2¼ cups)**
- ½ **cup water**
- 1 **teaspoon salt**
- 1 **to 1½ teaspoons chili powder**
- ¼ **teaspoon pepper**
- ¼ **cup uncooked barley**

In 3-quart saucepan, cook and stir meat and onion until meat is brown and onion is tender. Drain off fat. Stir in remaining ingredients; heat to boiling. Reduce heat, cover and simmer until barley is done and stew is desired consistency, about 1 hour. *2 servings*.

VELVET CRUMB CAKE WITH PINEAPPLE SAUCE

⅓ cup brown sugar (packed)
2 teaspoons cornstarch
1 can (8½ ounces) crushed pineapple
2 servings Velvet Crumb Cake
    (page 86) or pound cake
    or 2 commercially prepared sponge shortcakes

Mix sugar and cornstarch in small saucepan. Stir in pineapple (with syrup). Cook over medium heat, stirring constantly, until mixture thickens and boils. Boil and stir 1 minute. Serve warm sauce on cake. Top with whipped topping or whipped cream if you like. *2 servings.*

**Skillet Macaroni and Cheese
Scalloped Tomatoes
Marinated Green Bean Salad (page 104)
Hard Rolls
Gingerbread Stacks with Hot Butterscotch Sauce**

SKILLET MACARONI AND CHEESE

    3   tablespoons butter or margarine
    ½   package (7.25-ounce size) macaroni and Cheese*
    2   tablespoons chopped green pepper
 1½   cups hot water
    ½   to ¾ cup cubed cooked ham or pork luncheon meat
    ½   teaspoon dry mustard
    2   tablespoons chopped pimiento, if desired

Melt butter in 8-inch skillet. Cook and stir macaroni
and green pepper over medium heat until macaroni is
light golden, 3 to 5 minutes. Stir in water. Cover and
simmer until macaroni is tender, about 15 minutes. Stir
in meat, Sauce Mix and mustard. Simmer, stirring
constantly, until meat is hot and cheese sauce is thickened, about 2 minutes. Stir in pimiento. *2 servings*.

*To use half the package, measure contents and divide
in half (approximately ¾ cup macaroni and 2 tablespoons Sauce Mix). To store remaining mix, close
package securely and use within 2 weeks.

SCALLOPED TOMATOES

    1 can (8 ounces) stewed tomatoes
    ⅛ teaspoon salt
    ⅛ teaspoon sugar
       Dash pepper
    1 teaspoon butter or margarine
    ⅓ cup seasoned croutons

In small saucepan, heat tomatoes, salt, sugar and pepper to boiling. Reduce heat; cover and simmer 5 minutes. Stir in butter, sprinkle croutons on top. *2 servings*.

GINGERBREAD STACKS
WITH HOT BUTTERSCOTCH SAUCE

    ½ package (14.5-ounce size) gingerbread mix*
    ½ cup lukewarm water
    ¼ cup butterscotch ice-cream topping
       Vanilla ice cream

Heat oven to 350°. Grease and flour loaf pan, 9x5x3 inches. In small mixer bowl, mix gingerbread mix and lukewarm water on low speed. Beat on medium speed 2 minutes scraping bowl frequently, or beat 300 strokes by hand. Pour into pan. Bake until wooden pick inserted in center comes out clean, 15 to 20 minutes.

    Heat butterscotch topping. Cut 2 servings from gingerbread; split each piece. Fill layers with ice cream; top with hot butterscotch topping. *2 servings*.

* ½ package is approximately 1½ cups. To store remaining mix, close package securely and use within 3 weeks to make hot gingerbread. Or make the entire package at one time and freeze leftover gingerbread for use as needed.

**Deep-dish Hamburger Pie
Cabbage Slaw (page 33)
Garlic Bun Sticks
Cherry-Berry Parfaits**

*When your dimes have to roll up their sleeves,
hamburger can be a valiant helper. Especially in
a quick-to-the-oven dish like this. Of course,
you've made dessert ahead, so you simply sit back
and relax.*

DEEP-DISH HAMBURGER PIE

½ **pound ground beef**
¼ **cup chopped onion**
¼ **teaspoon salt**
⅛ **teaspoon pepper**
¼ **teaspoon monosodium glutamate**
1 **can (8 ounces) cut green beans, drained**
½ **can (10¾-ounce size) condensed tomato soup or
½ cup catsup**
1 **cup mashed potatoes**
3 **tablespoons shredded natural Cheddar cheese**

Heat oven to 350°. In 8-inch skillet, cook and stir meat
and onion until meat is brown and onion is tender. Stir
in seasonings, beans and soup. Pour into ungreased
1-quart casserole. Spoon mashed potatoes on mixture
and top with cheese. Bake until mixture is hot and top
is slightly brown, about 30 minutes. *2 servings*.

Note: Leftover mashed potatoes can be used in this
recipe. Or prepare instant mashed potatoes as directed
on package for 2 servings.

GARLIC BUN STICKS

Heat oven to 350°. Brush soft butter or margarine on 1 split frankfurter bun or 2 slices bread. Sprinkle with garlic salt and cut into strips. Place on ungreased baking sheet. Bake until golden brown, about 15 minutes. *2 servings*.

CHERRY-BERRY PARFAITS

- 1 cup boiling water
- 1 package (3 ounces) cherry- or strawberry-flavored gelatin
- 1 package (10 ounces) frozen strawberries
- ¼ cup cold water

Pour boiling water on gelatin in bowl; stir until gelatin is dissolved. Stir in frozen strawberries until thawed. Stir in cold water. Chill until thickened but not set, about 1½ hours.

Pour 1½ cups of the gelatin mixture into bowl; beat until light and fluffy. (Use remaining gelatin mixture as suggested below.) Divide between parfait glasses or dessert dishes. Chill until set, about 1 hour. Garnish with a dollop of whipped topping. *2 servings*.

Note: You can use the remaining gelatin mixture for tomorrow's salad. Divide between 2 individual molds and chill until set. Or serve as a dessert if you like: Pour remaining gelatin mixture into small shallow container and chill until set. Cut gelatin into cubes and layer in parfait glasses with vanilla pudding or frozen whipped topping (thawed).

Country-fried Chicken
Pan Gravy
Mashed Potatoes
Green Peas
Lemon-Fresh Mushroom Salad
Peach-Praline Shortcake (page 79)

COUNTRY-FRIED CHICKEN

   Salad oil
¼ **cup all-purpose flour**
½ **teaspoon salt**
⅛ **teaspoon pepper**
⅛ **teaspoon paprika**
1½ **pounds chicken pieces or 2-pound broiler-fryer chicken, quartered or cut up**

Heat ¼ inch salad oil in large skillet. Mix flour, salt, pepper and paprika; coat chicken with flour mixture. Cook chicken in oil over medium heat until light brown, 15 to 20 minutes. Reduce heat; cover tightly and simmer until thickest pieces are tender, 20 to 25 minutes, turning chicken once or twice to assure even cooking. (Add small amount of water if necessary.) Remove cover the last 5 minutes of cooking time to crisp chicken. *2 servings.*

PAN GRAVY

 1 **tablespoon drippings (fat and juices)**
 1 **tablespoon flour**
 ½ to ¾ **cup liquid (broth, milk, vegetable liquid, water)**
   Salt and pepper

Remove meat to warm platter; keep warm while preparing gravy. Pour drippings into bowl, leaving brown particles in pan. Return 1 tablespoon drippings to pan. Mix in flour. Cook over low heat, stirring until mixture is smooth and bubbly. Remove from heat. Stir in liquid. Heat to boiling, stirring constantly. Boil and stir 1 minute. If desired, stir in few drops bottled brown bouquet sauce for color. Season with salt and pepper. *½ to ¾ cup*.

SOMETHING TO KNOW ABOUT...

When you stir flour into pan drippings to make Pan Gravy, make sure you scrape in all the brown particles formed by cooking the meat—they're full of flavor and will give the gravy a deep-brown color. Don't forget that Pan Gravy can be made with the drippings of any meat that's been panfried, oven roasted or broiled, from pork chops to the Thanksgiving turkey.

LEMON-FRESH MUSHROOM SALAD

¼ **pound fresh mushrooms, sliced**
   Lemon-Herb Marinade (below)
2 **lettuce wedges**
2 **large tomato slices**

Place mushrooms in glass dish. Pour Lemon-Herb Marinade on mushrooms; cover and refrigerate up to 12 hours. Place lettuce wedge with tomato slice on each salad plate and top with mushrooms and small amount of marinade. *2 servings*.

Lemon-Herb Marinade

¼ **cup salad oil**
¼ **cup lemon juice**
1 **teaspoon seasoned salt**
¼ **teaspoon marjoram, basil or oregano**
⅛ **teaspoon sugar**
⅛ **teaspoon garlic salt**
   Dash freshly ground pepper

Shake all ingredients together in tightly covered jar. *½ cup*.

Split Pea Soup
Assorted Crackers
Lettuce Wedges with Waldorf Dressing
Spicy Raisin Cake with Browned Butter Frosting

SPLIT PEA SOUP

    2 cups dried split peas
    2 quarts water
    1 pound smoked ham shank or ham hocks or 1 ham
       bone
    1 medium onion, finely chopped (about ½ cup)
    1 cup finely chopped celery
    1 sprig parsley
    ¼ teaspoon pepper
    2 medium carrots, thinly sliced

In large saucepan or Dutch oven, heat peas and water
to boiling; boil 2 minutes. Remove from heat; cover
and let stand 1 hour.

Add ham shank, onion, celery, parsley and pepper;
heat to boiling. Reduce heat; cover and simmer 1½
hours. Add carrots; cover and simmer until carrots are
done and soup is of desired consistency, about 30
minutes.

Remove bone; trim meat from bone and add meat to
soup. For a thinner consistency, stir milk or water into
soup. Season to taste.

Serve half the soup for this meal. Refrigerate remaining soup for the next day. Or pour soup into
freezer container and freeze. *2 servings—and 2 for
another day.*

LETTUCE WEDGES WITH WALDORF DRESSING

- ½ cup diced unpared red apple
- ¼ cup seeded Tokay grape halves
- 2 tablespoons chopped celery
- ½ cup blue cheese dressing or mayonnaise
  Lettuce wedges

Mix apple, grapes, celery and dressing; spoon on lettuce wedges. *2 servings.*

SPICY RAISIN CAKE

- 1¼ cups all-purpose flour*
- 1 cup sugar
- 1½ teaspoons baking powder
- 1 teaspoon cinnamon
- ½ teaspoon salt
- ½ teaspoon nutmeg
- ¼ teaspoon cloves
- ¾ cup milk
- ⅓ cup shortening
- 1 egg
- 1 cup raisins
  Browned Butter Frosting (at right)

Heat oven to 350°. Grease and flour baking pan, 8x8x2 or 9x9x2 inches. Into larger mixer bowl, measure all ingredients except raisins and frosting. Blend on low speed ½ minute, scraping bowl constantly. Beat on high speed 3 minutes, scraping bowl occasionally. Fold in raisins. Pour into pan. Bake until wooden pick inserted in center comes out clean, 35 to 40 minutes. Cool; frost with Browned Butter Frosting.

* If using self-rising flour, omit baking powder and salt.

Browned Butter Frosting

    3 tablespoons butter
1 ½ cups confectioners' sugar
    ½ teaspoon vanilla
        About 1 tablespoon milk

In small saucepan, heat butter over medium heat until a delicate brown. Mix into sugar. Stir in vanilla and milk until frosting is smooth and of spreading consistency. *Enough frosting for an 8- or 9-inch square cake.*

Variation

Spicy Raisin Cupcakes: Place paper baking cups in 15 or 16 muffin cups. Pour batter into cups, filling each ½ full. Bake 25 to 30 minutes.

Garlic-Chip Chicken
Quick Scalloped Potatoes
Skillet Asparagus
Cranberry Relish Salad
Brownies à la Mode

GARLIC-CHIP CHICKEN

¼ cup shortening (part butter) or salad oil
1 teaspoon garlic salt
⅛ teaspoon pepper
1½ pounds chicken pieces or 2-pound broiler-fryer
    chicken, quartered
1 bag (3½ ounces) potato chips, crushed (about 1½
    cups)

Heat oven to 400°. In oven, melt shortening with garlic
salt and pepper in baking pan, 9x9x2 inches. Dip
chicken into shortening to coat all sides, then roll in
potato chips. Place skin side down in pan. Bake uncovered 30 minutes. Turn; bake until thickest pieces
are tender, about 30 minutes. *2 servings*.

QUICK SCALLOPED POTATOES

Heat oven to 400°. Measure contents of 1 package (5.5 ounces) scalloped potatoes; divide in half (approximately 1 cup potato slices and 3 tablespoons sauce mix).* Place half the potato slices in ungreased 2½-cup or 1-quart casserole. Sprinkle 3 tablespoons sauce mix on slices. Stir in half the amounts of butter, water and milk called for on package. Bake uncovered until potatoes are tender and golden brown, 25 to 30 minutes. *2 generous servings.*

* To store remaining mix, close package securely and use within 2 weeks to make Scalloped Potatoes with Ham (page 144).

SKILLET ASPARAGUS

Break off tough ends of ¾ to 1 pound asparagus as far down as stalks snap easily. Wash asparagus and remove scales if sandy or tough. Fill 10-inch skillet ⅓ full with water; add ½ teaspoon salt and heat to boiling. Add asparagus; heat to boiling. Cover and cook until stalk ends are crisp-tender, 8 to 12 minutes. Drain; return asparagus to skillet to dry. Dot with 1 tablespoon butter or margarine. *2 servings.*

CRANBERRY RELISH SALAD

    1 cup boiling water
    1 package (3 ounces) lemon-flavored gelatin
    1 package (10 ounces) frozen cranberry-orange relish
      Lettuce

Pour boiling water onto gelatin in bowl; stir until gelatin is dissolved. Stir in frozen relish until thawed. Pour into 4-cup mold or 4 to 6 individual molds. Chill until firm. Place 2 servings on lettuce; if desired, top with mayonnaise. Serve remaining gelatin topped with whipped cream as dessert the next day. *2 servings— and 2 or more for another day.*

Note: Pineapple-flavored gelatin can be substituted for the lemon-flavored gelatin. And for variety, add one of the following: 1 can (8¼ counces) crushed pineapple (with syrup); 1 apple, chopped; ⅓ cup chopped nuts.

BROWNIES À LA MODE

Bake 1 package (15 ounces) fudge brownie mix as directed. For each serving, place scoop of vanilla, coffee or peppermint ice cream on brownie square. Heat ¼ cup chocolate fudge sauce; drizzle on ice cream.

Broiled Fish and Taters
Buttered Peas
Cabbage Slaw (page 33)
Brown Beauty Cake with Fudge Frosting

BROILED FISH AND TATERS

1 pound fresh or frozen cod, perch or flounder fillets
2 tablespoons butter or margarine, melted
1 tablespoon lemon juice
2 tablespoons catsup
½ teaspoon Worcestershire sauce
½ teaspoon salt
⅛ teaspoon dry mustard
2 cooked pared medium potatoes, cut into ⅜-inch slices
2 tablespoons butter or margarine, melted
3 tablespoons grated Parmesan cheese

Thaw fillets if frozen; cut into serving pieces. Set oven control at broil and/or 550°. Place fish on greased rack in broiler pan. Mix 2 tablespoons butter, the lemon juice, catsup, Worcestershire sauce, salt and mustard; brush part of sauce on fish. Broil fish with tops 4 inches from heat 8 minutes, brushing with sauce once or twice. Turn fish; brush with remaining sauce. Arrange potato slices on broiler rack. Brush 2 tablespoons butter on potatoes and sprinkle with cheese. Broil until fish flakes easily with fork and potatoes are golden brown, about 5 minutes. *2 servings*.

Time-saver: No cooked potatoes on hand—and no time to cook them? Use ½ package (14-ounce size) frozen sliced panfried or French fried potatoes instead.

BROWN BEAUTY CAKE

1 **cup all-purpose flour* or cake flour**
1 **cup sugar**
½ **teaspoon soda**
½ **teaspoon salt**
¼ **teaspoon baking powder**
¼ **cup water**
½ **cup buttermilk**
¼ **cup shortening**
1 **egg**
½ **teaspoon vanilla**
2 **ounces melted unsweetened chocolate (cool)**
Fudge Frosting (at right)

Heat oven to 350°. Grease and flour baking pan, 8x8x2 or 9x9x2 inches. Into large mixer bowl, measure all ingredients except Fudge Frosting. Blend on low speed ½ minute, scraping bowl constantly. Beat on high speed 3 minutes, scraping bowl occasionally. Pour into pan.

Bake until wooden pick inserted in center comes out clean, 30 to 35 minutes. Cool. Frost with Fudge Frosting.

*If using self-rising flour, omit soda, salt and baking powder.

Fudge Frosting

- ¼ cup shortening
- 1 cup sugar
- 2 squares (1 ounce each) unsweetened chocolate
- ⅓ cup milk
- ¼ teaspoon salt
- 1 teaspoon vanilla

In 2-quart saucepan, heat all ingredients except vanilla to rolling boil, stirring occasionally. Boil 1 minute without stirring. Place pan in bowl of ice and water; beat frosting until cool and of spreading consistency. Stir in vanilla. *Enough frosting for 8- or 9-inch square cake.*

Chicken Cacciatore
Spaghetti
Zucchini Parmesan
Fresh Spinach Salad
Rainbow Parfaits

CHICKEN CACCIATORE

    Salad oil
  ¼ cup all-purpose flour
  ½ teaspoon salt
  ⅛ teaspoon pepper
  ⅛ teaspoon paprika
  1 to 1½ pounds chicken pieces or 2-pound broiler-fryer chicken, cut up
  1 jar (15 ounces) meatless spaghetti sauce
  1 can (2 ounces) mushroom stems and pieces
  ¼ teaspoon instant minced garlic
  1 teaspoon parsley flakes
  ¼ cup sliced pitted ripe olives
3½ to 4 ounces uncooked spaghetti

Heat ⅛ inch salad oil in large skillet. Mix flour, salt, pepper and paprika; coat chicken with flour mixture. Cook chicken in oil over medium heat until light brown, 15 to 20 minutes. Mix spaghetti sauce, mushrooms (with liquid), garlic, parsley flakes and olives. Drain fat from skillet. Pour sauce onto chicken. Heat to boiling. Reduce heat; cover tightly and simmer until thickest pieces of chicken are tender, about 30 minutes.

    While chicken simmers, cook spaghetti as directed on package. Drain. Serve chicken with spaghetti. *2 servings*.

ZUCCHINI PARMESAN

Cut 1 medium zucchini into strips, 2x½ inch. Heat 1 inch salted water (½ teaspoon salt to 1 cup water) to boiling. Add zucchini. Cover and heat to boiling; cook until tender, 7 to 9 minutes. Drain. Add 1 tablespoon butter or margarine and toss. Sprinkle 1 tablespoon grated Parmesan cheese on zucchini. *2 servings*.

FRESH SPINACH SALAD

> **2 cups bite-size pieces spinach leaves
> (about 5 ounces)**
> **2 green onions, sliced
> Seasoned salt**
> **2 tablespoons imitation bacon**
> **2 tablespoons oil-and-vinegar dressing**

Divide spinach between salad bowls. Sprinkle onion slices, seasoned salt and imitation bacon on spinach. Drizzle 1 tablespoon dressing on each serving. If you like, garnish with lemon twists. *2 servings*.

RAINBOW PARFAITS

Choose 2 or 3 flavors sherbet, such as raspberry, pineapple and/or lime (about ½ pint each). Make balls with scoop or spoon. Divide between parfait glasses and place in freezer.

At serving time, fill glasses with ginger ale, and if desired, garnish each with whipped topping. *2 servings*.

Dixie Bake with Buttermilk Biscuits
Succotash
Cranberry-Pineapple Salad
Chocolate-Cinnamon Ice Cream

DIXIE BAKE WITH BUTTERMILK BUSCUITS

     1 can (12 ounces) pork luncheon meat
    12 whole cloves
    ¼ cup apricot preserves
     1 teaspoon water
    ¼ teaspoon dry mustard
     1 cup buttermilk baking mix
    ¼ cup water

Heat oven to 425°. Score top of meat, cutting 12
squares or diamonds 1 inch deep. Insert clove in each
square. Place meat in ungreased baking pan, 8x8x2
inches. pushing meat to one side of pan. Mix preserves, 1 teaspoon water and the mustard; spoon on
meat.

Stir baking mix and ¼ cup water with fork to a soft
dough. Turn onto floured cloth-covered board; smooth
dough into ball and knead 5 times. Roll dough ½ inch
thick. Cut into five 2-inch biscuits; place in pan with
meat. Bake until biscuits are golden brown and meat is
hot, 15 to 20 minutes. *2 servings*.

Time-Saver: Forget all about kneading and rolling the
dough. Instead, drop by spoonfuls (5) right into the
pan.

SUCCOTASH

½ package (10-ounce size) frozen corn and lima beans
¼ teaspoon salt
Dash pepper
2 tablespoons light cream
1 tablespoon butter or margarine

Cook corn and lima beans as directed except—use only half the amounts of water and salt called for on package. Drain. Add remaining ingredients; heat, stirring occasionally, until butter is melted. *2 servings.*

CRANBERRY-PINEAPPLE SALAD

1 can (8 ounces) jellied cranberry sauce, cut into
  ¼-inch slices
1 can (8½ ounces) sliced pineapple, drained
  Crisp salad greens

Arrange cranberry and pineapple slices on salad greens. Serve with mayonnaise or salad dressing if you like. *2 servings.*

Variation

Cranberry-Orange Salad: Substitute 1 orange, pared and cut into ¼-inch slices, for the pineapple.

CHOCOLATE-CINNAMON ICE CREAM

Soften 1 pint chocolate ice cream slightly; stir in ½ teaspoon cinnamon. Spoon ice cream into original container, refrigerator tray or dessert dishes and freeze until firm. *2 servings.*

Chili con Carne
Cucumber-Iceberg Salad
Ripe Olives
Cornmeal Butter Sticks
Pineapple Pudding

Riddle: How do you turn hot chili into a frozen asset? Easy. Simply double the recipe and stash half in the freezer as a head start for another meal. There's time, while the chili cooks, to turn out the butter sticks, toss the salad and stir up the pudding dessert. Then for a quick chill, pop the dessert dishes in the freezer until ready to serve. All set? Turn on a South-of-the-Border record to give your dinner an appropriate accent.

CHILI CON CARNE

 ½ pound ground beef
 1 medium onion, chopped (about ½ cup)
 ½ cup chopped green pepper
 1 can (16 ounces) tomatoes
 1 can (8 ounces) tomato sauce
 1 teaspoon salt
 1 to 2 teaspoons chili powder
   Dash cayenne red pepper
   Dash paprika
 1 can (8 ounces) kidney beans

In 8-inch skillet, cook and stir meat, onion and green pepper until meat is brown and onion is tender. Drain off fat. Stir in remaining ingredients except beans. Heat to boiling. Reduce heat; cook uncovered about 30 minutes. Stir in beans (with liquid); heat until bubbly. *2 servings.*

CUCUMBER-ICEBERG SALAD

1½ cups shredded iceberg lettuce
½ medium cucumber, cut into cubes
Grated Parmesan cheese
Oil-and-vinegar dressing

Toss lettuce and cucumber cubes in bowl; sprinkle cheese on top. Serve with dressing. *2 servings*.

CORNMEAL BUTTER STICKS

¼ cup butter or margarine
½ cup buttermilk baking mix
½ cup cornmeal
¼ cup water
Salt

Heat oven to 450°. In oven, melt butter in baking pan, 9x9x2 inches. Stir baking mix, cornmeal and water with fork to soft dough. Turn onto floured cloth-covered board; smooth dough into ball and knead 5 times. Roll into rectangle, 6x4 inches. Cut into 8 strips, 4x¾ inch.

Dip each strip into melted butter, coating all sides, and arrange in pan. Sprinkle salt lightly on strips. Bake until golden brown, 12 to 15 minutes. Serve hot. *8 sticks*.

PINEAPPLE PUDDING

1 can (8¼ ounces) crushed pineapple, drained
½ can (17.5-ounce size) vanilla pudding (1 cup)
Toasted coconut

Fold pineapple into pudding; divide between dessert dishes. Chill. Top each serving with coconut. *2 servings*.

Sausage and Sauerkraut with Dumplings
Fresh Vegetable Relishes
Warm Rye Rolls
Spiced Applesauce à la Mode
Gingersnaps

*Sometimes the very simplest of meals is the most
memorable. Especially one with such pungent,
old-world fragrance and hearty goodness. All
this and "cents-ible" besides! After the robust
main dish, you'll like the contrast of a light,
refreshing dessert, just tweaked with spicy
overtones.*

SAUSAGE AND SAUERKRAUT WITH DUMPLINGS

  1 can (8 ounces) sauerkraut
  4 medium Polish or bratwurst sausages
 ¼ teaspoon caraway seed
  1 tablespoon chopped onion
 ½ cup water
 ½ cup buttermilk baking mix
  3 tablespoons milk
     Snipped parsley

In saucepan, heat sauerkraut (with liquid), sausages,
caraway seed, onion and water to boiling. Reduce
heat; cover and simmer 30 minutes.

Stir baking mix and milk with fork to a soft dough.
Drop dough by spoonfuls (2 or 3) onto sauerkraut.
Cook uncovered over low heat 10 minutes; cover and
cook 10 minutes. Remove dumplings, sausages and
sauerkraut with slotted spoon to serving platter. Garnish with parsley. *2 servings.*

FRESH VEGETABLE RELISHES

Arrange a variety of vegetables attractively on small tray or in mug. Suggestions include: cherry tomatoes; carrot, cucumber, celery or zucchini sticks; green or red pepper strips or rings. Or prepare any of the vegetable relishes below. Chill until serving time.

Broccoli Buds and Cauliflowerets: Break head of broccoli or cauliflower into bite-size flowerets.

Carrot Curls: With vegetable parer, cut carrot lengthwise into paper-thin slices. Roll up slices and fasten with picks. Place in ice and water. (Remove picks before serving.)

Cucumber Petals: Run tines of fork down length of unpared cucumber. Cut crosswise into very thin slices.

Green Onions: Remove any loose layers of skin. Trim, leaving about 3 inches of green.

Radish Fans: Remove stem and root ends from large radishes. Make thin crosswise cuts almost through radishes. Place in ice and water.

Rutabaga or Turnip Strips: Thinly pare raw rutabaga or turnip; cut into narrow strips or thin slices. For an attractive design, use a lattice cutter.

SPICED APPLESAUCE À LA MODE

  1 cup applesauce
  ½ teaspoon cinnamon
  ½ teaspoon lemon juice
     Vanilla ice cream

In small saucepan, heat applesauce, cinnamon and lemon juice, stirring occasionally, until hot. Divide applesauce between dessert dishes. Top each serving with ice cream. *2 servings.*

**Frankfurters
Hot German Potato Salad
Buttered Green Beans
Cherry Skillet Cobbler**

FRANKFURTERS

Drop 4 large frankfurters (about ¾ pound) into boiling water. Cover; reduce heat and simmer until heated through, 5 to 8 minutes. Remove frankfurters from water with tongs. *2 servings.*

HOT GERMAN POTATO SALAD

  2 **medium potatoes, pared and halved**
  3 **slices bacon**
  ⅓ **cup chopped onion**
  1 **tablespoon flour**
  2 **teaspoons sugar**
  ¾ **teaspoon salt**
  ¼ **teaspoon celery seed**
    Dash pepper
  ⅓ **cup water**
  3 **tablespoons vinegar**

Heat 1 inch salted water (½ teaspoon salt to 1 cup water) to boiling. Add potatoes. Cover and heat to boiling; cook until tender, 20 to 25 minutes. Drain and set aside.

In 8-inch skillet, fry bacon until crisp; remove and drain. In same skillet, cook and stir onion in bacon fat until tender. Stir in flour, sugar, salt, celery seed and pepper. Cook over low heat, stirring until mixture is bubbly. Remove from heat. Stir in water and vinegar. Heat to boiling, stirring constantly. Boil and stir 1 minute. Remove from heat.

Crumble bacon into hot mixture, then slice warm potatoes into hot mixture. Cook until hot and bubbly, stirring lightly to coat potato slices. *2 servings*.

BUTTERED GREEN BEANS

Cook ½ package (9-ounce size) frozen cut green beans as directed except—use only half the amounts of water and salt called for on package. Drain. Dot with 1 tablespoon butter or margarine and sprinkle with chopped salted peanuts, sunflower seeds or almonds. *2 servings*.

CHERRY SKILLET COBBLER

  ½ can (21-ounce size) cherry pie filling
  ¼ cup orange juice
  ½ cup buttermilk baking mix
  1 tablespoon shredded orange peel, if desired
1½ teaspoons sugar
  2 tablespoons milk

In 1-quart saucepan, heat pie filling and orange juice to boiling, stirring occasionally. Stir baking mix, orange peel, sugar and milk with fork to a soft dough. Drop dough by spoonfuls (2 or 3) onto boiling cherry mixture. Cook uncovered over low heat 10 minutes; cover and cook 10 minutes longer. Serve warm. Top with light cream or ice cream if you wish. *2 servings*.

EVERYDAY FAVORITES
Dinners that make tried-and-true
seem suddenly new

Salmon Loaf
Lemon-buttered Broccoli
Fresh Fruit Salad with Lime-Honey Dressing
Breadsticks
Hot Fudge Pudding Cake

SALMON LOAF

    1 can (8 ounces) salmon, drained (reserve liquid)
      Milk plus reserved salmon liquid to measure ⅓ cup
    1 egg, slightly beaten
    ¾ cup cracker crumbs
    1 tablespoon lemon juice
    1 tablespoon chopped onion
      Dash pepper
      Egg Sauce (at right)

Heat oven to 350°. Flake salmon, removing skin and
bone. Mix in remaining ingredients except sauce. In
buttered baking pan, 8x8x2 inches, shape mixture into
a loaf. Bake uncovered until center is firm, about 30
minutes. Serve with Egg Sauce. *2 servings*.

74

Egg Sauce

1 **tablespoon butter or margarine**
1 **tablespoon flour**
¼ **teaspoon salt**
⅛ **teaspoon pepper**
¾ **cup milk**
1 **hard-cooked egg, diced**

Melt butter in small saucepan. Mix in flour, salt and pepper. Cook over low heat, stirring until mixture is smooth and bubbly. Remove from heat and stir in milk. Heat to boiling, stirring constantly. Boil and stir 1 minute. Stir in egg. *¾ cup.*

Variations

Cucumber Sauce: Omit egg and stir in ¼ cup shredded or thinly sliced cucumber and dash cayenne red pepper.

Dill Sauce: Omit egg and stir in ½ teaspoon dill weed and dash nutmeg.

LEMON-BUTTERED BROCCOLI

Heat oven to 350°. In ungreased 1-quart casserole, place 1 package (10 ounces) frozen broccoli spears, 1 tablespoon butter or margarine and 2 teaspoons lemon juice. Cover and bake until tender, about 35 minutes. *2 servings.*

FRESH FRUIT SALAD

    1 grapefruit, pared and sectioned
    ¼ cantaloupe, pared and cut into pieces
    1 cup fresh strawberries, halved
       Lime-Honey Dressing (page 106)
       Lettuce

Toss fruit and dressing. Serve salad on lettuce. *2 servings*.

HOT FUDGE PUDDING CAKE

    ⅓ cup all-purpose flour*
    ¼ cup granulated sugar
    1 tablespoon cocoa
    ¾ teaspoon baking powder
    ⅛ teaspoon salt
    3 tablespoons milk
    1 tablespoon salad oil
    ⅓ cup chopped nuts
    ⅓ cup brown sugar (packed)
    1 tablespoon cocoa
    ⅔ cup hot water.

Heat oven to 350°. Mix all ingredients except brown sugar, 1 tablespoon cocoa and the hot water. Pour into ungreased 1-quart casserole. Mix brown sugar and 1 tablespoon cocoa; sprinkle on batter. Pour hot water on batter. Bake 30 to 35 minutes. Serve warm. Top with whipped cream or ice cream if you wish. *2 servings*.

*If using self-rising flour, omit baking powder and salt.

**Oven-fried Chicken
Parsleyed New Potatoes
Asparagus Almondine
Crisp Vegetable Relishes
Strawberry Shortcake**

*Crisp, crusty fried chicken that really isn't fried
at all. It's baked! No tiresome tending and, best
of all, no spattering. And since the shortcakes
bake at the same temperature, they can share the
oven toward the end. Now, that's teamwork.*

OVEN-FRIED CHICKEN

¼ cup shortening (part butter) or salad oil
¼ cup all-purpose flour
½ teaspoon salt
⅛ teaspoon paprika
⅛ teaspoon pepper
1½ pounds chicken pieces or 2-pound broiler-fryer
     chicken, cut into quarters.

Heat oven to 425°. In oven, melt shortening in baking
pan, 9×9×2 inches or 11¾×7½×1½ inches. Mix
flour, salt, paprika and pepper in plastic or paper bag;
shake chicken, 2 or 3 pieces at a time, in bag until
coated.

Place chicken skin side down in pan. Bake uncovered 30 minutes. Turn chicken; bake until tender,
15 to 20 minutes longer. *2 servings.*

PARSLEYED NEW POTATOES

 1 **pound new potatoes (6 to 8 small)**
 2 **tablespoons butter or margarine**
 1 **to 2 tablespoons snipped parsley**

Scrub unpared potatoes lightly with vegetable brush.
Heat 1 inch salted water (1 teaspoon salt to 1 cup water)
to boiling. Add potatoes. Cover and heat to boiling;
cook until tender, 20 to 25 minutes. Drain. Add butter;
toss until potatoes are coated. Sprinkle with parsley. *2
servings*.

ASPARAGUS ALMONDINE

 1 **package (10 ounces) frozen asparagus spears**
 1 **tablespoon butter or margarine**
 2 **tablespoons diced roasted almonds**

Cook asparagus spears as directed on package. Drain.
Turn into serving dish; dot with butter and sprinkle
almonds on top. *2 servings*.

STRAWBERRY SHORTCAKE

    1 pint fresh strawberries
    ⅓ to ½ cup sugar
    1 cup buttermilk baking mix
    ¼ cup milk
    1 tablespoon sugar
    1 tablespoon butter or margarine, melted

Slice strawberries into bowl. Sprinkle ⅓ to ½ cup sugar on berries and let stand about 1 hour.

Heat oven to 425°. Mix remaining ingredients with fork to a soft dough. Turn dough onto lightly floured cloth-covered board; smooth dough into ball and knead 8 to 10 times. Roll ½ inch thick. Cut into two 3-inch circles. Place on ungreased baking sheet. Bake 10 to 12 minutes.

Split warm shortcakes; spoon strawberries between layers and on top. Serve with sweetened whipped cream if desired. *2 servings*.

Variation

Peach-Praline Shortcake: Omit strawberries and sugar. Before baking, brush soft butter or margarine on circles; sprinkle brown sugar on tops. Fill and top shortcakes with sweetened sliced peaches.

Meat Loaf
Creamy Scalloped Potatoes
Fresh Vegetables Vinaigrette (page 121)
Peach Crisps

MEAT LOAF

- 1 egg
- ½ cup milk
- ⅓ cup dry bread crumbs or 1 cup soft bread crumbs (about 1½ slices bread, torn into small pieces)
- 1 pound ground beef or meat loaf mixture
- 2 tablespoons finely chopped onion
- ½ teaspoon salt
- ⅛ teaspoon pepper
- ¼ teaspoon dry mustard
- ¼ teaspoon garlic salt
- 1 teaspoon Worcestershire sauce

Mix all ingredients thoroughly. Divide meat mixture in half (about 1½ cups each); shape each into loaf, 5×4 inches. Place both loaves in ungreased loaf pan, 9×5×3 inches, or baking pan, 9×9×2 inches.

Bake in 350° oven about 45 minutes. If desired, top one loaf with catsup, chili sauce or strips of cheese and return to oven for 2 to 3 minutes. Serve this loaf immediately. Cool remaining loaf; wrap in aluminum foil, label and freeze. *2 servings—and 2 for another time.*

Note: To serve frozen meat loaf, place foil-wrapped *frozen* loaf on oven rack; heat in 350° oven 50 to 60 minutes.

CREAMY SCALLOPED POTATOES

    2 tablespoons butter or margarine
    2 tablespoons flour
    ½ teaspoon salt
    ⅛ teaspoon pepper
    1½ cups milk
    1 pound potatoes (about 3 medium), pared and thinly
       sliced
    2 tablespoons finely chopped onion
    1 teaspoon butter or margarine

Heat oven to 350°. Melt 2 tablespoons butter over low heat. Stir in flour and seasonings. Cook over low heat, stirring until smooth and bubbly. Remove from heat. Stir in milk. Heat to boiling, stirring constantly.

In greased 1-quart casserole, layer half the potatoes, all the onion and half the sauce. Top with remaining potatoes and sauce. Dot with 1 teaspoon butter.

Cover and bake 30 minutes. Uncover and bake until potatoes are tender, about 35 minutes. *2 servings.*

PEACH CRISPS

    4 canned peach halves, drained
    2 tablespoons chopped walnuts
    2 tablespoons brown sugar
    1½ teaspoons finely shredded orange peel
    ⅛ teaspoon allspice
    4 walnut halves

Heat oven to 350°. Place peach halves cut sides up in ungreased baking dish. Mix chopped walnuts, sugar, orange peel and allspice; sprinkle on peaches. Bake until hot, about 20 minutes. Serve warm; top each with walnut half and, if desired, vanilla ice cream. *2 servings.*

Baked Meatballs
Oven Rice
Spanish Peppers
Cabbage Slaw (page 33)
Quick Blueberry Cobbler

*Time for a change? The meat loaf mix on page 80
can be a whole new "ball" game if you fix half
loaf, half meatballs. (Either will keep frozen up to
2 months.) Note the change in procedure, too.
These meatballs bake in the oven—no watching,
no stirring, no spattering.*

BAKED MEATBALLS

Prepare mixture for Meat Loaf (page 80) except—
decrease milk to ¼ cup. Shape mixture into twenty
1½-inch balls. Place in ungreased baking pan, 9x9x2
inches. Bake in 400° oven about 20 minutes. Serve half
the meatballs immediately. Cool remaining meatballs;
place in 1-pint freezer container, label and freeze.
2 servings—and 2 for another day.

Note: To serve frozen meatballs, heat 1 jar (about 15
ounces) favorite spaghetti sauce in 1-quart saucepan to
boiling; add frozen meatballs. Reduce heat; cover and
simmer until meatballs are hot, about 20 minutes.
Serve with hot cooked spaghetti or noodles. Or heat 1
can (10¾ ounces) beef gravy to boiling; add frozen
meatballs and heat through. Serve with mashed potatoes.

OVEN RICE

   1 **cup boiling water**
   ½ **cup uncooked regular rice**
   ½ **teaspoon salt**
      Snipped parsley

Heat oven to 400°. Mix water, rice and salt in un-greased 2½-cup or 1-quart casserole. Cover tightly; bake until liquid is absorbed and rice is tender, 20 to 25 minutes. Sprinkle parsley on top. *1½ cups rice.*

SPANISH PEPPERS

   1 **to 1½ green peppers, cut into ½ inch strips**
   ½ **cup ¼-inch diagonal slices celery**
   2 **tablespoons finely chopped onion**
   1 **tablespoon salad oil**
   ¼ **teaspoon basil leaves**
   ½ **teaspoon salt**
      Dash pepper
   1 **can (8 ounces) tomato sauce**

In 8-inch skillet, cook and stir green pepper, celery and onion in oil over medium heat until onion is tender. Stir in remaining ingredients. Cover and cook over medium heat until green pepper is crisp-tender, about 5 minutes. *2 servings.*

QUICK BLUEBERRY COBBLER

- ½ can (21-ounce size) blueberry pie filling*
- ½ teaspoon shredded orange peel
- ½ cup buttermilk baking mix
- 2 teaspoons sugar
- 2 tablespoons orange juice
- 2 teaspoons butter or margarine, softened

Heat oven to 400°. Mix pie filling and orange peel in ungreased 2½-cup casserole. Heat in oven 15 minutes. Stir baking mix, sugar, orange juice and butter with fork to soft dough. Drop dough by spoonfuls (2 or 3) onto hot blueberry mixture. Bake until topping is light brown 15 to 20 minutes. Serve warm, with light cream or ice cream if you like. *2 servings*.

***Leftover pie filling?** Serve in tart shells or use as a topping for vanilla ice cream, lemon sherbet, vanilla pudding, pancakes or French toast.

Lamb Chops Hawaiian
Fluffy White Rice
Minted Carrots
Tossed Spinach Salad (page 39)
Velvet Crumb Cake with Broiled Topping

Lamb chops don't have to deal your budget a body blow. Not if you look for cuts from the shoulder. And taste what a hint of mint (traditional with lamb) can do to rouse carrots out of the ho-hum category. Another time use mint to perk up peas.

LAMB CHOPS HAWAIIAN

   2 lamb shoulder chops (arm or blade), ½ inch thick
   1 can (8¼ ounces) pineapple chunks, drained
       (reserve syrup)
   2 tablespoons soy sauce
   2 tablespoons vinegar
   ¼ teaspoon dry mustard
   1 tablespoon salad oil
   2 tablespoons brown sugar
   ¾ teaspoon cornstarch
1½ cups hot cooked rice
       Parsley

Place meat in shallow glass dish. Mix reserved pineapple syrup, the soy sauce, vinegar and mustard; pour on meat. Cover and refrigerate at least 4 hours, turning meat occasionally.

Remove meat from marinade; reserve marinade. Heat oil in 8-inch skillet; brown meat over medium heat. Pour ¼ cup reserved marinade on chops. Cover and simmer until tender, 30 to 40 minutes.

Mix sugar and cornstarch in small saucepan. Stir in remaining reserved marinade. Heat to boiling, stirring constantly. Reduce heat; simmer 2 to 3 minutes. Stir in pineapple; heat through, about 1 minute. Serve chops with pineapple sauce and rice. Garnish with parsley. *2 servings*.

MINTED CARROTS

   4 or 5 medium carrots
   1 tablespoon mint-flavored jelly or 1 teaspoon finely snipped mint leaves

Cut carrots lengthwise into ⅛-inch-wide strips. Heat 1 inch salted water (½ teaspoon salt to 1 cup water) to boiling. Add carrots. Cover and heat to boiling; cook until tender, about 10 minutes. Drain. Dot hot carrots with jelly; stir lightly to glaze carrots. *2 servings*.

VELVET CRUMB CAKE WITH BROILED TOPPING

Bake Velvet Crumb Cake as directed on package of buttermilk baking mix. Spread Broiled Topping (at right) on ⅓ of warm cake. Cover remaining cake with aluminum foil. Broil cake with top 3 inches from heat until topping is golden, about 3 minutes. *2 servings*.

Broiled Topping

    2 tablespoons brown sugar
    2 tablespoons soft butter or margarine
    1 tablespoon half-and-half
    ¼ cup coconut
    2 tablespoons chopped nuts

Mix all ingredients.

Note: Wrap remaining cake in aluminum foil (2 servings in each package) and store in refrigerator or freezer. To serve warm, heat in foil in 400° oven 10 minutes (if frozen, heat 30 to 35 minutes). Top with apricot or peach jam, cranberry relish, blueberry or cherry pie filling, fresh or frozen (thawed) strawberries, Pineapple Sauce (page 47) or vanilla ice cream and chocolate sauce.

> **French Onion Soup**
> **Shrimp Creole**
> **Fluffy White Rice**
> **Tossed Green Salad**
> **French Bread**
> **Southern Ambrosia**
> **Praline Squares**

SHRIMP CREOLE

  2 **tablespoons butter or margarine**
  ¾ **cup chopped onion**
  ½ **cup chopped celery**
  1 **medium green pepper, chopped (about ½ cup)**
  1 **small clove garlic, minced, or ⅛ teaspoon instant minced garlic**
  1 **can (8 ounces) tomato sauce**
  ½ **cup water**
  1 **teaspoon parsley flakes or snipped parsley**
  ½ **teaspoon salt**
  ⅛ **teaspoon cayenne red pepper**
  1 **bay leaf, crushed**
  1 **package (7 ounces) frozen cleaned raw shrimp* (about 1 cup)**
1½ **cups hot cooked rice**

Melt butter in 8-inch skillet; cook and stir onion, celery, green pepper and garlic over medium heat until onion is tender. Stir in tomato sauce, water, parsley flakes and seasonings. Simmer uncovered 20 minutes, stirring occasionally. Stir in frozen shrimp; heat to boiling. Reduce heat; cover and simmer until shrimp are done, about 10 minutes. Serve on rice. *2 servings*.

*Rinse frozen shrimp under running cold water to remove ice glaze before adding to sauce.

SOUTHERN AMBROSIA

Sprinkle confectioners' sugar and flaked coconut on orange slices.

PRALINE SQUARES

¼ cup shortening or salad oil
1 cup brown sugar (packed)
1 egg
1 teaspoon vanilla
¾ cup all-purpose flour*
1 teaspoon baking powder
½ teaspoon salt
½ cup chopped nuts

Heat oven to 350°. Grease baking pan, 8×8×2 inches. Melt shortening in saucepan over low heat. Remove from heat; mix in sugar, egg and vanilla. Stir in remaining ingredients. Spread in pan. Bake 25 minutes. While warm, cut into 2-inch squares. *16 squares.*

*If using self-rising flour, omit baking powder and salt.

SOMETHING TO KNOW ABOUT ...

For every 1 cup cleaned cooked shrimp your recipe calls for, you can
 prepare 1 package (7 ounces) frozen peeled shrimp or ...
 prepare ¾ pound fresh or frozen raw shrimp (in shells) or ...
 use 1 can (4½ or 5 ounces) shrimp.

Sweet-and-Sour Ribs
Baked Acorn Squash
Chinese-style Cabbage
Rosy Cinnamon Apples

SWEET-AND-SOUR RIBS

2 pounds pork spareribs or back ribs, cut into
   serving pieces
½ cup catsup
2 tablespoons brown sugar
¼ cup vinegar
2 tablespoons Worcestershire sauce
1 teaspoon celery seed
½ teaspoon chili powder
½ teaspoon salt
   Dash pepper
2 to 3 drops red pepper sauce

Place ribs meaty side up on rack in foil-lined shallow
roasting pan. Mix remaining ingredients; pour about ⅓
cup sauce on ribs. Bake uncovered in 350° oven until
done, 1½ to 2 hours, basting 3 or 4 times with remaining sauce.

For additional flavor and eye appeal, place 1 lemon,
thinly sliced, on ribs during last hour of baking. If ribs
are browning too quickly, cover loosely with aluminum foil. *2 servings*.

Variation

Pineapple Ribs: Decrease vinegar to 2 tablespoons
and add 1 can (8 ounces) crushed pineapple (with
syrup) to the sauce ingredients.

BAKED ACORN SQUASH

Heat oven to 350°. Cut 1 acorn squash lengthwise in half. Place cut sides down in ungreased baking dish, 8×8×2 inches. Pour water into baking dish to ¼-inch depth. Bake uncovered 30 minutes. Turn squash cut sides up. Dot each half with butter or margarine; sprinkle with salt, pepper, and if desired, 1 tablespoon brown sugar or honey. Bake until squash is tender, 20 to 30 minutes. *2 servings*.

CHINESE-STYLE CABBAGE

```
   1   tablespoon salad oil
1 ½   cups finely shredded cabbage
   ½   cup thin diagonal slices celery
   ½   medium green pepper, cut into thin diagonal slices
   ⅓   cup chopped onion
   ½   teaspoon salt
        Dash pepper
```

Heat oil in 8-inch skillet; add vegetables and mix. Cover tightly and cook over medium-low heat, stirring occasionally, just until crisp-tender, 3 to 5 minutes. Sprinkle with salt and pepper. For extra flavor, add 1½ teaspoons soy sauce just before serving. *2 servings*.

ROSY CINNAMON APPLES

Heat oven to 350°. Core 2 baking apples. Pare upper half of each apple to prevent skin from splitting. Or score skin in petal design. Place apples upright in small baking dish; fill center of each with 1 to 2 tablespoons brown sugar and 1 tablespoon red cinnamon candies. Pour water into baking dish to ¼-inch depth. Bake until apples are tender when pierced with fork, 30 to 40 minutes, spooning syrup on apples several times during baking. Serve warm, with cream or ice cream. *2 servings*.

Herbed Halibut Steaks
Baked Potatoes
Asparagus Pimiento
Crisp Vegetable Relishes
Strawberries and Cream

HERBED HALIBUT STEAKS

- 1 tablespoon butter or margarine
- 2 tablespoons lemon juice
- 1 package (12 ounces) frozen halibut steaks
- 1 teaspoon onion salt
- ¼ teaspoon lemon pepper
- ¼ to ½ teaspoon thyme, basil or marjoram
  Paprika
  Lemon wedges
  Parsley

Heat oven to 400°. In oven, melt butter in lemon juice in baking pan, 8×8×2 inches. Place frozen fish in pan; turn to coat other side with lemon butter. Sprinkle onion salt, lemon pepper and thyme on fish. Bake until fish flakes easily with fork, about 25 minutes. Sprinkle paprika on fish; serve with lemon wedges and parsley. *2 servings*.

BAKED POTATOES

Heat oven to 400°. Rub 2 medium baking potatoes with shortening if soft skins are desired. Prick with fork to allow steam to escape. Bake until tender, about 1 hour.

To serve, cut crisscross gash in each top; squeeze gently until some potato pops up through opening. Serve with butter or dairy sour cream. *2 servings*.

Orange Pork Chop Skillet
Buttered Peas
Tossed Green Salad
Dinner Rolls
Quick Date Cake

ORANGE PORK CHOP SKILLET

4 pork loin or rib chops, ½ to ¾ inch thick
1 teaspoon salt
1 small onion, sliced
½ can (6-ounce size) frozen orange juice concentrate (thawed)*
2 tablespoons brown sugar
¼ teaspoon allspice
2 tablespoons lemon juice
2 tablespoons water
1 can (8 ounces) sweet potatoes in syrup, drained
1 small orange, sliced

In 10-inch skillet, brown chops over medium heat. Drain off fat. Sprinkle salt on chops. Arrange onion slices on chops. Mix orange juice concentrate, sugar, allspice, lemon juice and water; pour into skillet. Heat to boiling. Reduce heat; cover and simmer 30 minutes. Place sweet potatoes and orange slices on chops. Cover and cook until potatoes are hot, about 10 minutes. *2 servings.*

*Leftover concentrate? Use in Orange Slush (page 27), as an ice-cream topping or for a speedy fruit drink.

TOSSED GREEN SALAD

  3 to 4 cups bite-size pieces chilled crisp salad greens
  ¼ cup vegetables
     **Oil-and-Vinegar Dressing (below) or favorite
     bottled dressing**

Place greens and vegetables in bowl. Just before serving, pour dressing on ingredients and toss. Garnish salad as desired. *2 servings*.

Oil-and-Vinegar Dressing

  2 tablespoons salad oil
  **1 tablespoon wine, tarragon or cider vinegar or lemon
     juice**
  ¼ teaspoon salt
  **½ small clove garlic, finely chopped, or dash garlic
     powder**
     Dash freshly ground pepper

Shake all ingredients in tightly covered jar. *About ¼ cup*.

Note: For perfect green salads, use chilled fresh salad greens. Vary the greens, vegetables and garnishes. Tear greens into bite-size pieces; do not cut except when wedges, shredding or chunks are called for. Use just enough dressing to lightly coat the leaves.

QUICK DATE CAKE

- 1 **package (14 ounces) date bar mix**
- ½ **cup hot water**
- 2 **eggs**
- 1 **teaspoon baking powder**
- ½ **cup chopped walnuts**
  Confectioners' sugar

Heat oven to 375°. Grease baking pan, 8×8×2 inches. Mix date filling from date bar mix and hot water. Stir in crumbly mix, eggs, baking powder and nuts. Spread in pan. Bake until top springs back when touched lightly, about 30 minutes. Sprinkle confectioners' sugar on top.

Southwestern Beef
Buttered Green Beans
Tangy Cauliflower Salad
Quick Corn Muffins
Caramel Custard or Frosty Pumpkin Custard

SOUTHWESTERN BEEF

¾- to 1-pound beef round steak, 1 to 2 inches thick
2 cloves garlic, thinly sliced
1 tablespoon salad oil
½ teaspoon salt
Dash marjoram or basil
¼ cup water
1 tablespoon butter or margarine
⅓ cup raisins
1 large or 2 small tomatoes, peeled and cut into wedges
Pickled chili peppers

Cut about 10 small slits in meat with tip of knife; insert a garlic slice in each. Heat oil in 8-inch skillet; brown meat over medium heat, about 15 minutes. Drain off fat. Add salt, marjoram and water; heat to boiling. Reduce heat; cover tightly and simmer until tender, 1 to 1½ hours. (Add small amount of water if necessary.)

Melt butter in small saucepan. Add raisins and tomatoes; cook over low heat, stirring occasionally, until hot, about 5 minutes. Pour around steak and garnish with chili peppers. *2 servings*.

TANGY CAULIFLOWER SALAD

½ **medium cauliflower**
2 **tablespoons oil-and-vinegar dressing**
¼ **teaspoon oregano**
¼ **teaspoon salt**
   Lettuce leaves

Separate cauliflower into flowerets. Heat 1 inch salted water (½ teaspoon salt to 1 cup water) to boiling. Add cauliflower. Cover and heat to boiling; cook until tender, 10 to 12 minutes. Drain.

Mix dressing, oregano and salt; pour on hot cauliflower and toss. Cover and refrigerate at least 3 hours.

To serve, remove cauliflower with slotted spoon to lettuce-lined bowls. Garnish with finely chopped green onion or grated Parmesan cheese and parsley. *2 servings.*

Time-saver: Substitute 1 package (10 ounces) frozen cauliflower, cooked as directed, for the fresh.

QUICK CORN MUFFINS

Measure 1 package (14 ounces) corn muffin mix; divide in half (approximately 1½ cups).* Prepare muffins as directed except—use half the mix, 1 egg and half the amount of milk called for on package. *6 muffins.*

* To store remaining mix, close package securely and use within 3 weeks to make hot muffins for another meal. Or if you prefer, prepare entire package and freeze leftover muffins to use as needed.

CARAMEL CUSTARD

> 1 egg, slightly beaten
> 2 tablespoons sugar
>   Dash salt
> ½ teaspoon vanilla
> ¾ cup milk, scalded
> 2 tablespoons caramel ice-cream topping

Heat oven to 350°. Mix egg, sugar, salt and vanilla. Stir in milk. Place 1 tablespoon caramel topping in each of two 6-ounce custard cups. Pour egg mixture onto caramel topping.

Place cups in baking pan, 8x8x2 inches; pour very hot water into pan to within ½ inch of tops of cups. Bake until knife inserted halfway between center and edge comes out clean, 40 to 45 minutes. Remove cups from water; serve warm or chill and unmold into dessert dishes. *2 servings*.

FROSTY PUMPKIN CUSTARD

Line 6 muffin cups with paper baking cups. Soften ½ pint vanilla ice cream slightly. Fold ½ can (16-ounce size) pumpkin pie mix* into ice cream. Divide among paper-lined cups. Cover and freeze until firm, at least 3 hours. Garnish with whipped topping and walnut halves. *2 servings—and 4 for other days*.

*Leftover pumpkin pie mix? Use in Pumpkin Custards (page 155).

Hearty Ham Steak
Grilled Sweet Potatoes
Peas Almondine in Foil
Corn Muffins from the Grill
Banana Boats

HEARTY HAM STEAK

2 tablespoons prepared mustard
2 tablespoons pineapple juice or other fruit juice
1 tablespoon brown sugar
1 teaspoon horseradish
  Dash salt
1 fully cooked ham slice, about ¾ inch thick.

Combine all ingredients except ham slice in small saucepan; heat to boiling, stirring occasionally.

Place ham on grill 4 inches from medium coals. Cook until hot and glazed, about 5 minutes on each side, basting frequently with mustard mixture. *2 servings.*

GRILLED SWEET POTATOES

Pare 2 sweet potatoes; cut diagonally into ½-inch slices. Cook slices in 1 inch boiling water 10 minutes. Drain. Mix 2 tablespoons butter or margarine, melted, and ¼ teaspoon salt.

Place potato slices on grill 4 inches from medium coals. Cook 10 minutes on each side, brushing frequently with butter mixture. Sprinkle toasted coconut on potato slices. *2 servings.*

PEAS ALMONDINE IN FOIL

   1 package (10 ounces) frozen green peas
   2 tablespoons slivered almonds
      Salt and pepper
   1 tablespoon butter or margarine
   1 teaspoon chopped pimiento, if desired

Place frozen block of peas on 18-inch square of double thickness heavy-duty aluminum foil. Sprinkle almonds, salt and pepper on peas. Dot with butter. Wrap securely in foil. Cook directly on medium coals, turning once, until tender, 18 to 20 minutes. Add pimiento just before serving. *2 servings*.

CORN MUFFINS FROM THE GRILL

Bake Quick Corn Muffins (page 98) ahead of time. Split and butter each muffin. Wrap in double thickness heavy-duty aluminum foil. Heat on grill 4 inches from medium coals until hot, about 10 minutes, turning once.

BANANA BOATS

For each serving, cut V-shaped wedge lengthwise in a peeled firm banana. Place on piece of double thickness heavy-duty aluminum foil, 18×6 inches. Fill groove in banana with miniature or cut-up marshmallows and chocolate pieces. Wrap tightly in foil. Cook directly on medium coals about 10 minutes.

Puffy Omelet Cahuenga
Maple-glazed Bacon
Marinated Green Bean Salad
Toasted English Muffins
Fresh Fruit Cup

PUFFY OMELET CAHUENGA

Puffy Omelet (at right)
1   **ripe small avocado**
¾   **cup dairy sour cream**
½   **teaspoon salt**
⅛   **teaspoon dill weed**
1   **large tomato, peeled, diced and drained**

Prepare Puffy Omelet. While omelet bakes, peel and dice avocado. Heat sour cream, salt and dill weed (do not boil). Gently stir tomato and avocado into sour cream mixture; heat through.

To serve, pour part of the sauce on omelet in skillet. Tip skillet and loosen omelet by slipping rubber scraper, pancake turner or spatula under; fold omelet and remove to heated platter. Pour remaining sauce on top. *2 generous servings.*

Puffy Omelet

    3 eggs, separated
    3 tablespoons milk or water
    ¼ teaspoon salt
    ⅛ teaspoon pepper
    1 tablespoon butter or margarine

In small mixer bowl, beat egg whites until stiff but not dry. Beat egg yolks until thick and lemon colored. Beat in milk, salt and pepper; gently fold into egg whites with rubber scraper.

Heat oven to 325°. In 8-inch skillet with ovenproof handle, heat butter until just hot enough to sizzle a drop of water, rotating skillet so that butter evenly coats the bottom. Pour omelet mixture into skillet; level surface gently. Reduce heat; cook until puffy and light brown on bottom, about 5 minutes. (Lift omelet at edge to judge color.)

Place skillet in oven; bake until knife inserted in center comes out clean, 12 to 15 minutes.

Note: To make a perfect puffy omelet, gently fold the egg yolk mixture into the stiffly beaten egg whites with a rubber scraper. Don't overfold, or you'll deflate the mixture.

Cook the omelet on top of the range until it's puffy and the bottom is light brown, lift the edge to judge the color. It then goes into the oven to bake until it's done.

Fill the omelet with part of the sauce. Tip the skillet and fold the omelet in half. Slide it onto a platter and pour the remaining sauce on top.

MAPLE-GLAZED BACON

 ½ **pound Canadian-style bacon, cut into ¼-inch slices**
 2 **tablespoons maple-flavored syrup**

Heat oven to 325°. In ungreased small shallow baking
dish, overlap bacon slices slightly. Drizzle syrup on
slices. Bake uncovered until bacon is hot, about 35
minutes. *2 servings*.

MARINATED GREEN BEAN SALAD

Drain liquid from 1 can (8 ounces) French-style green
beans. Pour 2 tablespoons Italian dressing on beans.
Cover and refrigerate at least 2 hours. Drain. Serve
beans on crisp salad greens and garnish with onion
rings. *2 servings*.

FRESH FRUIT CUP

Choose two or more of the following fruits to total 1 to
1½ cups: banana slices; blueberries; strawberries;
raspberries; seedless green grapes; peach, pear or pineapple chunks; orange or grapefruit sections or melon
cubes. Divide between dessert dishes and top each
with ¼ cup orange juice or ginger ale. *2 servings*.

Swiss Steak
Mashed Potatoes
Buttered Brussels Sprouts
Apple-Grapefruit Salad
with Lime-Honey Dressing
Hard Rolls
Pecan Tarts

SWISS STEAK

¾- pound beef round steak, ½ to ¾ inch thick
2 tablespoons flour
¼ teaspoon salt
⅛ teaspoon pepper
2 tablespoons salad oil
1 can (8 ounces) stewed tomatoes
1 medium green pepper, sliced
1 medium onion, sliced
½ teaspoon salt

Cut meat into 2 pieces. Mix flour, ¼ teaspoon salt and the pepper; coat meat with flour mixture. Heat oil in 8-inch skillet; brown meat over medium heat, about 15 minutes. Add tomatoes to skillet. Reduce heat; cover and simmer 30 minutes. Add green pepper, onion and ½ teaspoon salt. Cover and simmer until meat is tender, 30 to 45 minutes. (Add small amount water if necessary.) *2 servings*.

APPLE-GRAPEFRUIT SALAD

Arrange unpared red apple slices and grapefruit sections on salad greens. Serve with Lime-Honey Dressing (below).

Lime-Honey Dressing

   3 tablespoons frozen limeade or
     lemonade concentrate (thawed)*
   3 tablespoons honey
   3 tablespoons salad oil or dairy sour cream
   ¼ teaspoon celery seed

Beat all ingredients until well blended. *½ cup.*

*Leftover concentrate? use in Lime Frappé (page 9), or Fresh Fruit Salad (page 76), drizzle it over a fruit cup or stir up a quick fruit drink.

PECAN TARTS

   ½ stick pie crust mix
   1 egg
   ¼ cup sugar
   ⅛ teaspoon salt
   3 tablespoons butter or margarine, melted
   ⅓ cup dark corn syrup
   ⅓ cup pecan halves or pieces

Heat oven to 375°. Prepare pastry for One-crust Pie as directed except—use only half the amount of water called for on package and divide dough in half. Roll each half 1 inch larger than 4-inch tart pan. Ease into pan; flute edge. (Do not prick.)

In small mixer bowl, beat egg, sugar, salt, butter and syrup. Stir in nuts. Pour into pastry-lined tart pans. Bake until filling is set and pastry is light brown, 30 to 35 minutes. Serve warm or cool. Top with whipped cream if desired. *2 tarts*.

No 4-inch tart pans? Use 1 stick or ½ packet pie crust mix. Prepare pastry for One-crust Pie as directed on package except—divide dough into 6 equal parts. Shape each into a ball and roll into 4½-inch circle. Ease into muffin cup or 6-ounce custard cup, making pleats so pastry will fit closely. (Do not prick.) Pour filling into pastry-lined muffin cups. Bake about 30 minutes.

Tuna Salad in Tomato Cups
Fresh Vegetable Relishes (page 71)
Popovers
Orange-Pineapple Ice Cream

TUNA SALAD IN TOMATO CUPS

  1 **can (6½ ounces) tuna, drained and separated into chunks**
  ¼ **cup chopped celery**
  2 **tablespoons chopped green pepper**
  1 **tablespoon finely chopped onion**
  ½ **teaspoon lemon juice**
  ½ **teaspoon soy sauce**
     Dash white pepper
  ¼ **cup mayonnaise or salad dressing**
  2 **medium tomatoes**
     Salt
  ⅓ **cup chow mein noodles or shoestring potatoes**
     Celery leaves
     Crisp salad greens

Toss tuna, celery, green pepper, onion, lemon juice, soy sauce, pepper and mayonnaise in bowl. Cover and chill.

Remove stem ends of tomatoes. Place tomatoes cut sides down; cut each into sixths, cutting to within 1 inch of bottom. Spread sections apart to form cups. Sprinkle salt on sections.

Fold noodles into tuna mixture. Spoon salad into tomato cups. Garnish cups with celery leaves and place on salad greens. *2 servings.*

POPOVERS

   1 egg
   ½ cup milk
   ½ cup quick-mixing flour*
   ¼ teaspoon salt

Heat oven to 450°. Grease generously 3 deep custard cups (6-ounce size) or 4 medium muffin cups. Beat egg slightly with fork; add milk, flour and salt and stir with fork just until smooth. Do not overbeat.

   Fill custard cups ½ full, muffin cups ¾ full. Bake 20 minutes. Lower oven temperature to 350° and bake until deep golden brown, about 20 minutes longer. Immediately remove popovers from cups; serve hot with butter. *3 or 4 popovers*.

*If using regular all-purpose flour, beat ingredients with rotary beater.

ORANGE-PINEAPPLE ICE CREAM

Soften 1 pint vanilla ice cream slightly. Stir in ½ can (6-ounce size) frozen orange-pineapple juice concentrate (thawed). Spoon ice cream into original container or refrigerator tray and freeze until firm. *2 servings*.

Variations

   Cinnamon Ice Cream: Substitute 1 teaspoon cinnamon for the concentrate.

   Coffee Ice Cream: Substitute 1 to 2 teaspoons powdered instant coffee for the concentrate.

   Nesselrode Ice Cream: Substitute 2 tablespoons Nesselrode for the concentrate.

Lemon Barbecued Pork Chops
Corn on the Cob
Lettuce Wedges with Roquefort Dressing
Hot Rolls
Apple Crisp

LEMON BARBECUED PORK CHOPS

      2 pork loin or rib chops, ¾ to 1 inch thick
     ½ teaspoon salt
      2 thin slices onion
      2 thin slices lemon
      2 tablespoons brown sugar
      2 tablespoons catsup

Heat oven to 350°. Trim excess fat from chops. Place
chops in ungreased baking pan, 8x8x2 inches; season
with salt. Top each chop with 1 slice onion, 1 slice
lemon, 1 tablespoon sugar and 1 tablespoon catsup.
Cover tightly with aluminum foil and bake 30 minutes.
Uncover; baste chops and bake until done, about 30
minutes. *2 servings*.

CORN ON THE COB

In large saucepan, heat enough water to boiling to
cover 2 to 4 ears corn. Do not add salt—salt toughens
corn. If desired, add 1 teaspoon sugar and 1 teaspoon
lemon juice for each 2 quarts water. Drop corn carefully into boiling water. Cover and cook 5 to 8 minutes, depending on size of corn. Drain. Serve with
butter, salt and pepper. For variety, try one of these
other favorite seasonings mixed with soft butter: basil,
cayenne red pepper, celery seed, chili powder or rosemary leaves. *2 servings*.

LETTUCE WEDGES WITH ROQUEFORT DRESSING

- ½ cup dairy sour cream
- ¼ cup crumbled Roquefort or blue cheese (about 1 ounce)
- ½ teaspoon lemon juice
- ¼ teaspoon salt
- 2 lettuce wedges

Mix all ingredients except lettuce wedges. Cover and refrigerate at least 1 hour to blend flavors. Add small amount milk or light cream if necessary for proper consistency. Spoon onto lettuce wedges. *2 servings*.

APPLE CRISP

- 2 cups sliced pared tart apples (2 medium)
- 1 tablespoon water
- ½ teaspoon lemon juice
- ½ teaspoon cinnamon
- ¼ cup granulated sugar or brown sugar (packed)
- 3 tablespoons flour
- 2 tablespoons butter or margarine

Heat oven to 350°. Place apple slices in ungreased 1¾-cup casserole. Sprinkle water, lemon juice and cinnamon on apples. Mix remaining ingredients until crumbly; sprinkle on apples. Bake uncovered until apples are tender and topping is golden brown, about 30 minutes. Serve warm. Top with light cream or ice cream if you like. *2 servings*.

Savory Beef Stew
Orange and Grapefruit Salad with
Ruby-red Dressing
Celery Sticks
Rye Rolls
Chocolate Chip Cookies

SAVORY BEEF STEW

 2 tablespoons shortening
 ½ to ¾ pound beef stew meat, cut into 1-inch pieces
1½ cups water
 1 beef bouillon cube
 ½ clove garlic, finely chopped, or ⅛ teaspoon instant
   minced garlic
 ½ bay leaf, crumbled
 1 teaspoon salt
 ⅛ teaspoon allspice
 ¼ teaspoon lemon juice
 2 small onions or 1 medium onion, cut into quarters
 2 medium potatoes, pared and cut into 1-inch cubes
 2 medium carrots, cut into 1-inch pieces
 ½ package (10-ounce size) frozen green peas*
 ½ cup water
 2 tablespoons flour

Melt shortening in 2-quart saucepan; brown meat. Add
1½ cups water, the bouillon cube, garlic, bay leaf,
salt, allspice and lemon juice; heat to boiling, stirring
occasionally. Reduce heat; cover and simmer until
meat is almost tender, 1 to 1½ hours.

Add onions, potatoes and carrots; heat to boiling.
Reduce heat; cover and simmer 20 minutes. Add peas;
cook until vegetables are tender, about 10 minutes.

Shake ½ cup water and the flour in tightly covered jar until smooth. Stir into stew; heat to boiling, stirring constantly. Boil and stir 1 minute. *2 generous servings*.

*Leftover frozen peas? Cook as directed on package and serve as the vegetable in Orange Pork Chop Skillet menu (page 94) or use in Peas Almondine in Foil (page 101) or Paella (page 118).

ORANGE AND GRAPEFRUIT SALAD

    1 orange, pared and sectioned
    1 grapefruit, pared and sectioned
      Crisp salad greens
      Ruby-red Dressing (below)

Arrange orange and grapefruit sections in pinwheel design on salad greens. Garnish with maraschino cherry if desired. Serve with Ruby-red Dressing. *2 servings*.

Ruby-red Dressing

Beat ¼ cup currant or cranberry jelly and 2 tablespoons oil-and-vinegar dresing until smooth.

Time-saver: Substitute 1 can (11 ounces) mandarin orange segments, drained, for the orange and grapefruit.

CHOCOLATE CHIP COOKIES

- ⅓ cup shortening
- ⅓ cup butter or margarine, softened
- ½ cup granulated sugar
- ½ cup brown sugar (packed)
- 1 egg
- 1 teaspoon vanilla
- 1½ cups all-purpose flour*
- ½ teaspoon soda
- ½ teaspoon salt
- ½ cup chopped nuts
- 1 package (6 ounces) semisweet chocolate pieces

Heat oven to 375°. Mix thoroughly shortening, butter, sugars, egg and vanilla. Stir in remaining ingredients. (For a softer, rounder cookie, add ¼ cup flour).

Drop dough by rounded teaspoonfuls 2 inches apart onto ungreased baking sheet. Bake until light brown, 8 to 10 minutes. Cool slightly before removing from baking sheet. *About 3½ dozen cookies*.

*If using self-rising flour, omit soda and salt.

Canadian-Style Bacon
Oven-baked Beans
Mixed Vegetable Salad
Date-Nut Bread
Baked Apples

CANADIAN-STYLE BACON

Place four to six ⅛-inch slices Canadian-style bacon (about ⅓ pound) in cold skillet. Cook over low heat, turning to brown evenly on both sides, 8 to 10 minutes. *2 servings*.

OVEN-BAKED BEANS

2 slices bacon, diced
1 small onion, sliced
1 can (16 ounces) baked beans with pork
2 tablespoons catsup or chili sauce
2 tablespoons brown sugar, if desired
1 teaspoon Worcestershire sauce
½ teaspoon prepared mustard

Heat oven to 350°. In large skillet, cook and stir bacon and onion until bacon is crisp. Drain off fat. Stir in remaining ingredients. Pour into ungreased 1-quart casserole. Bake uncovered until hot and bubbly, about 45 minutes. *2 servings*.

MIXED VEGETABLE SALAD

½ to 1 cup sliced or diced vegetables
    Oil-and-Vinegar Dressing (page 95)
    or 3 tablespoons Italian dressing
1 to 1½ cup bite-size pieces crisp salad greens

Marinate vegetables in dressing 1 to 2 hours. (Here are a few for-instances: raw zucchini, cucumbers, carrots or cauliflowerets; leftover cooked vegetables; canned peas, green beans or mixed vegetables.) Add salad greens and toss. *2 servings*.

DATE-NUT BREAD

½ cup boiling water
½ cup raisins
½ cup cut-up dates
1 tablespoon plus 1½ teaspoons butter or margarine
¾ teaspoon soda
¾ cup plus 2 tablespoons all-purpose flour*
½ cup sugar
¼ teaspoon salt
1 egg
½ teaspoon vanilla
¼ cup chopped nuts

Heat oven to 350°. Grease and flour 1-pound coffee can. Pour boiling water on raisins, dates, butter and soda; let stand until cool. Beat in remaining ingredients. Pour into coffee can. Bake until wooden pick inserted in center comes out clean, 60 to 65 minutes. Remove from can; cool thoroughly before slicing.

*If using self-rising flour, decrease soda to ¼ teaspoon and omit salt.

BAKED APPLES

Heat oven to 350°. Core 2 baking apples (such as Rome Beauty, Golden Delicious or Greening). Remove 1-inch strip of skin around middle of each apple or pare upper half of each to prevent skin from splitting.

Place apples upright in a small baking dish. Fill center of each apple with 1 to 2 tablespoons granulated or brown sugar, 1 teaspoon butter or margarine and ⅛ teaspoon cinnamon.

Pour water into baking dish to ¼-inch depth. Bake until apples are tender when pierced with fork, 30 to 40 minutes. (Time will vary with size and variety of apple.) If desired, spoon syrup in pan over apples several times during baking. *2 servings*.

Salted Almonds
Olives
Paella
Orange-Avocado Salad
Caramel Custard (page 99)
Sangría

PAELLA

2 tablespoons salad oil
1 to 1½ pounds chicken pieces
1 small onion, sliced
1 can (8 ounces) stewed tomatoes
1 teaspoon salt
1 teaspoon paprika
¼ teaspoon pepper
  Dash cayenne red pepper
½ package (6-ounce size) saffron rice (½ cup)
1½ cups chicken broth*
1 can (4½ ounces) medium shrimp,
  rinsed and drained
½ package (10-ounce size) frozen green peas,
  broken apart (about 1 cup)

Heat oil in Dutch oven; brown chicken. Remove chicken and set aside. Drain off fat.

Heat oven to 350°. Cook and stir onion, tomatoes and seasonings in Dutch oven until onion is tender, about 5 minutes. Stir in rice and broth; heat to boiling. Add chicken. Cover and bake 35 minutes. Add shrimp and peas; bake until chicken is tender, about 10 minutes. Serve in paella pan or shallow serving dish. Garnish with pimiento strips, parsley and artichoke hearts. *2 servings*.

Note: Saffron rice hard to come by? You can substitute ½ cup uncooked regular rice plus a dash of saffron or ⅛ teaspoon turmeric.

*Chicken broth can be made by dissolving 1 chicken bouillon cube in 1½ cups boiling water, or use canned chicken broth.

ORANGE-AVOCADO SALAD

    1 orange, pared and sliced
    1 avocado, pared and cut into wedges
    1 small onion, sliced and separated into rings
       Crisp salad greens
       Orange Dressing (below)

Arrange orange slices, avocado wedges and onion rings on salad greens. Drizzle Orange Dressing on salads. *2 servings*.

Orange Dressing

    ¼ cup salad oil
    1 tablespoon lemon juice
    ½ teaspoon grated orange peel
    2 tablespoons orange juice
    1 tablespoon sugar
    ⅛ teaspoon salt
    ⅛ teaspoon dry mustard

Shake all ingredients in tightly covered jar. *½ cup*.

Deluxe Baked Chicken
Chili Pepper Casserole
Fresh Vegetables Vinaigrette
Hot Crusty Rolls
Lemon Sherbet with Raspberry-Currant Sauce

DELUXE BAKED CHICKEN

  2 tablespoons salad oil
¼ cup all-purpose flour
½ teaspoon salt
¼ teaspoon paprika
⅛ teaspoon pepper
1½ pounds chicken pieces
¼ cup chicken broth
  2 tablespoons sherry or apple juice
  1 small clove garlic, crushed

Heat oil in large skillet. Measure flour, salt, paprika
and pepper into plastic or paper bag. Shake chicken, 2
or 3 pieces at a time, in bag until thoroughly coated.
Brown chicken in oil over medium heat.

Heat oven to 350°. Place chicken skin side up in
ungreased baking pan, 9x9x2 inches. Mix broth, sherry
and garlic. Pour ⅓ of broth mixture on chicken. Cover
with aluminum foil and bake until tender, 45 to 50
minutes, basting occasionally with remaining broth
mixture. Uncover last 5 minutes of baking time to crisp
chicken. *2 servings*.

CHILI PEPPER CASSEROLE

½ can (4-ounce size) peeled green chili peppers*
1 cup shredded process Cheddar cheese
  (about 4 ounces)
1 egg
½ cup milk
¼ cup buttermilk baking mix

Heat oven to 350°. Grease 2- to 2½-cup casserole. Rinse peppers to remove seeds. Place peppers in single layer in casserole. Sprinkle cheese on peppers. Beat egg thoroughly; beat in milk and baking mix and pour onto cheese. Bake until golden brown and puffy, about 30 minutes. *2 servings*.

*Leftover chili peppers? Chop and use as a spicy substitution for pimiento.

FRESH VEGETABLES VINAIGRETTE

1 small zucchini or cucumber, thinly sliced
1 carrot, cut crosswise into ¼-inch slices
¼ cup cauliflowerets
¼ cup oil-and-vinegar dressing
2 lettuce cups

Toss all ingredients except lettuce cups in bowl. Chill at least 2 hours, tossing occasionally. Serve in lettuce cups. *2 servings*.

LEMON SHERBET WITH RASPBERRY-CURRANT SAUCE

    1   package (10 ounces) frozen raspberries, thawed
    ½   cup currant jelly
    1½ teaspoons cornstarch
    1   tablespoon cold water
    ½   pint lemon sherbet

Heat raspberries (with syrup) and currant jelly to boiling, stirring frequently. Mix cornstarch and water until smooth. Stir into raspberry-currant mixture. Cook, stirring constantly, until mixture thickens and boils. Boil and stir 1 minute. Cool, and if desired, strain.

   Scoop sherbet into dessert dishes. Pour sauce on top. *2 servings*.

Note: Leftover sauce can be stored in refrigerator and served later in the week on ice cream or custard.

PLANNING
AHEAD

**Dinners that star a "big" meat buy—with
repeat performances as sparkling as First Night**

Roast Pork
Herbed Brussels Sprouts
Country-style Waldorf Salad
Dinner Rolls
Lemon Pudding Cake

ROAST PORK

Place roast fat side up on rack in shallow roasting pan.
Season with salt and pepper before, during or after
roasting (salt goes into roast only ¼ to ½ inch). Insert
meat thermometer so tip is in center of thickest part of
meat and does not touch bone or rest in fat.

Roast uncovered in 325° oven until done (see Timetable on page 124), using thermometer reading as final
guide. Roasts are easier to carve if allowed to "set" 15
to 20 minutes after removing from oven. Since meat
continues to cook after removal from oven, if roast is to
set, it should be removed from oven when thermometer registers 5° lower than the desired doneness.

TIMETABLE

Cut	Approximate Cooking Time (Minutes per Lb.)	Meat Thermometer Reading
Loin		
Center		
3 to 5 lbs.	30 to 35	170°
Blade		
5 to 7 lbs.	35 to 40	170°
Sirloin		
3 to 4 lbs.	40 to 45	170°
Boneless Top (double)		
3 to 5 lbs.	35 to 45	170°
Boneless Top		
2 to 4 lbs.	30 to 35	170°

HERBED BRUSSELS SPROUTS

Cook 1 package (10 ounces) frozen Brussels sprouts as directed. Drain. Add 1 tablespoon butter or margarine and ⅛ teaspoon dill weed, caraway seed or marjoram leaves and toss. *2 servings*.

COUNTRY-STYLE WALDORF SALAD

- ½ cup diced unpared apple (about ½ apple)
- ⅓ cup diced celery
- ¼ cup halved seedless green grapes
- 2 tablespoons coarsely chopped nuts
- 1 cup bite-size pieces lettuce
- ¼ cup mayonnaise or salad dressing

Toss all ingredients in bowl. Garnish salad with unpared apple slices. *2 servings*.

LEMON PUDDING CAKE

- 1 egg, separated
- 1 teaspoon grated lemon peel
- 2 tablespoons lemon juice
- ⅓ cup milk
- ½ cup sugar
- 2 tablespoons flour
- ⅛ teaspoon salt

Heat oven to 325°. Beat egg white until stiff peaks form. Beat egg yolk; add remaining ingredients and beat until smooth. Fold in egg white.

Divide between ungreased 1-cup baking dishes or 6-ounce custard cups. Place in pan of hot water (1 inch deep). Bake 45 to 50 minutes. Serve warm, with whipped cream if you like. *2 generous servings*.

Applause from the audience as pork stages a comeback. Star it in an Oriental show of chow mein or a speedy meal-in-a-skillet. And for a final bow, a casserole that calls for your can opener and oven to do most of the work.

CHINESE PORK AND RICE

⅓ cup uncooked regular rice
¼ cup chopped onion
1 stalk celery, cut into diagonal slices
1 tablespoon salad oil
¾ cup water
1 teaspoon instant chicken or beef bouillon
1 tablespoon soy sauce
1 cup cut-up cooked pork (¾-inch pieces)
½ green pepper, chopped

In 8-inch skillet, cook and stir rice, onion and celery in oil over medium heat until rice is golden brown and onion is tender. Stir in water, bouillon, soy sauce and meat; heat to boiling, stirring occasionally. Reduce heat; cover tightly and simmer until rice is tender, 12 to 15 minutes. Stir in green pepper; cover and simmer until liquid is absorbed and pepper is crisp-tender, about 5 minutes. *2 servings*.

PORK CHOW MEIN

- 1 tablespoon salad oil or shortening
- 1 to 1½ cups cubed cooked pork
- 1 small onion, chopped (about ¼ cup)
- 1 cup water
- 1 teaspoon instant chicken bouillon
- ¼ teaspoon garlic salt
- 1 can (about 3 ounces) sliced mushrooms, drained (reserve liquid)
- 1 tablespoon soy sauce
- 2 tablespoons cornstarch
- 1 can (16 ounces) Chinese vegetables, drained
  Chow mein noodles

Heat oil in 8-inch skillet; brown meat and push to one side. Add onion; cook and stir until onion is tender. Stir in water, bouillon and garlic salt; heat to boiling. Reduce heat; cover and simmer 5 minutes.

Blend reserved mushroom liquid, soy sauce and cornstarch; stir into meat mixture. Add mushrooms and Chinese vegetables. Cook, stirring constantly, until mixture thickens and boils. Boil and stir 1 minute. Serve on noodles, and if you like, with additional soy sauce. *2 servings*.

Variations

Beef, Chicken or Turkey Chow Mein: Substitute 1 to 1½ cups cubed cooked beef chicken or turkey for the pork.

SAUCY PORK 'N NOODLE BAKE

- 1 tablespoon salad oil
- 1 cup cut-up cooked pork
- ½ cup uncooked noodles
- 1 can (10½ ounces) condensed cream of chicken soup
- 1 can (8 ounces) whole kernel corn, drained
- 1 tablespoon sliced pimiento
- ½ cup shredded sharp Cheddar cheese
- ¼ cup finely diced green pepper

Heat oven to 375°. Heat oil in 8-inch skillet; brown meat over medium-high heat. Drain off fat. Stir in remaining ingredients. Pour into ungreased 1-quart casserole. Bake uncovered until noodles are tender, about 45 minutes. *2 generous servings.*

**Corned Beef and Cabbage with Horseradish Sauce
Anadama Batter Bread
Creamy Peach Pudding or Quick Mocha Dessert
Ginger Cookies**

CORNED BEEF AND CABBAGE

  2- to 3-pound beef corned brisket
  2 small onions
  4 small carrots
  2 small potatoes, pared and halved
  ½ green cabbage, cut into wedges
     Horseradish (below)

Cook meat as directed on package. If directions are not available, place meat in Dutch oven; cover with hot water. Heat to boiling. Reduce heat; cover tightly and simmer until tender, 3 to 3½ hours.

About 20 minutes before meat is tender, skim fat from liquid, then add onions, carrots and potatoes. Cover and simmer 20 minutes. Remove meat and keep warm.

Add cabbage to liquid; simmer uncovered until vegetables are tender, 10 to 15 minutes. To carve meat, cut thin diagonal slices across the grain. Serve with Horseradish Sauce. *2 servings*.

Horseradish Sauce

  ⅓ cup mayonnaise or dairy sour cream
  1 tablespoon horseradish
     Dash paprika
     Dash dry mustard

Mix all ingredients. Refrigerate until serving time. *About ⅓ cup*.

ANADAMA BATTER BREAD

¾ **cup boiling water**
½ **cup yellow cornmeal**
3 **tablespoons shortening**
¼ **cup molasses**
2 **teaspoons salt**
1 **package active dry yeast**
¼ **cup warm water (105 to 115°)**
1 **egg**
2¾ **cups all-purpose flour***

Grease loaf pan, 8½x4½x2¾ or 9x5x3 inches. In large mixer bowl, mix boiling water, the cornmeal, shortening, molasses and salt; cool to lukewarm.

Dissolve yeast in warm water. Add yeast, egg and half the flour to cornmeal mixture. Beat on medium speed 2 minutes, scraping bowl frequently, or beat 300 vigorous strokes by hand. Stir in remaining flour until smooth. Spread evenly in pan. Batter will be sticky; smooth top of loaf with floured hand.

Let rise in warm place until batter reaches top of 8½-inch pan or 1 inch from top of 9-inch pan, about 1½ hours. Sprinkle small amount of cornmeal and salt on loaf.

Heat oven to 375°. Bake until loaf sounds hollow when tapped, 50 to 55 minutes. Remove loaf from pan; place on wire rack. Brush top with melted butter or shortening. Cool before cutting. *1 loaf.*

*If using self-rising flour, omit salt.

Variations

Little Loaves: Grease 6 miniature loaf pans, 4½x 2½x1½ inches. Divide batter among pans and let rise until it just reaches the tops of the pans, about 1½ hours. Bake 30 to 35 minutes.

Oatmeal Batter Bread: Substitute ½ cup oats for the yellow cornmeal.

CREAMY PEACH PUDDING

½ can (17.5 ounce size) vanilla pudding (1 cup)
¼ cup dairy sour cream
1 can (8 ounces) sliced peaches, drained

Mix pudding and sour cream. Layer pudding and peaches in each dessert dish. *2 servings.*

QUICK MOCHA DESSERT

Blend ½ can (17.5-ounce size) chocolate pudding (1 cup) and 1½ teaspoons powdered instant coffee. Divide between dessert dishes and garnish with whipped topping and mint leaves. *2 servings.*

GINGER COOKIES

Heat oven to 375°. Mix 1 package (14.5 ounces) gingerbread mix and ½ cup water. Drop dough by teaspoonfuls about 2 inches apart onto lightly greased baking sheet. Bake until almost no imprint remains when touched, 10 to 12 minutes. *About 3 dozen cookies.*

Variation

Mincemeat Ginger Drops: Stir in 1 cup prepared mincemeat and ½ cup chopped nuts.

"Corned Beef Revisited": a clever variety show featuring robust Reuben sandwiches, a savory skillet hash, a reprise of corned beef and cabbage (only easier), a cheesy casserole (easier still).

CORNED BEEF AND MACARONI CASSEROLE

Heat oven to 375°. Measure contents of 1 package (7.25 ounces) macaroni and cheese; divide in half (approximately ¾ cup macaroni and 2 tablespoons Sauce Mix).*

In ungreased 1-quart casserole, mix half the macaroni, 2 tablespoons Sauce Mix, 1½ teaspoons butter or margarine and 1¼ cups boiling water. Stir in 1 cup cut-up cooked corned beef. Cover and bake 20 to 25 minutes. Stir before serving. *2 servings*.

*To store remaining mix, close package securely and use within 2 weeks. Delicious with hamburgers, frankfurters, chicken or luncheon meat.

Variations

Tuna and Macaroni Casserole: Omit corned beef and stir in 1 can (6½ ounces) tuna, drained and flaked.

Chicken and Macaroni Casserole: Omit corned beef and stir in 1 can (5 ounces) boned chicken, cut up, and 2 tablespoons sliced pimiento-stuffed olives.

REUBEN GRILL

2 tablespoons Thousand Island dressing
4 slices rye or pumpernickel bread
2 slices Swiss cheese
½ cup sauerkraut, drained
½ pound thinly sliced cooked corned beef
  Soft butter or margarine

Spread dressing on 2 slices bread. Top with cheese, sauerkraut, meat and remaining bread slices. Spread butter on outsides of sandwiches. Grill in skillet over low to medium heat until brown and cheese is melted, 5 to 7 minutes on each side. *2 servings*.

QUICK CORNED BEEF AND CABBAGE

2 tablespoons butter or margarine
1½ cups coarsely shredded cabbage
½ package (6-ounce size) hash brown potatoes
  with onions (about 1¼ cups)
¾ cup water
½ teaspoon salt
1 cup cut-up cooked corned beef

Melt butter in 8-inch skillet. Stir in cabbage, potatoes, water and salt. Cook over medium-high heat until liquid is absorbed and bottom is brown, 8 to 12 minutes. Sprinkle meat into skillet; turn mixture with wide spatula and cook until meat is hot, about 3 minutes. *2 servings*.

CORNED BEEF SKILLET HASH

- 1 cup chopped cooked corned beef
- 1 cup chopped cooked potatoes
- ¼ cup finely chopped onion
- 1 tablespoon snipped parsley
- ¼ teaspoon salt
- ⅛ teaspoon pepper
- 3 tablespoons salad oil
- ½ cup tomato juice

Mix meat, potatoes, onion, parsley, salt and pepper. Heat oil in 8-inch skillet. Spread meat mixture evenly in skillet; brown over medium heat, turning frequently with wide spatula, about 10 minutes. Stir in tomato juice. Reduce heat; cover and cook until liquid is absorbed, about 10 minutes. *2 servings*.

Mint-glazed Roast Lamb
Bulgur Pilaf
Spinach Soufflé (page 178)
Greek Salad (page 163)
Gourmet Pears

MINT-GLAZED ROAST LAMB

Place roast fat side up on rack in shallow roasting pan. Season with salt and pepper before, during or after roasting (salt goes into roast only ¼ to ½ inch). Insert meat thermometer so tip is in thickest part of meat and does not touch bone or rest in fat.

Roast uncovered in 325° oven to desired doneness (see Timetable below), using thermometer reading as final guide. During last hour of roasting, brush meat

TIMETABLE

Cut	Approximate Cooking Time (Minutes per Lb.)	Meat Thermometer Reading
Rolled Leg		
3 to 5 lbs.	35 to 40	175 to 180°
Leg		
5 to 6 lbs.	30 to 35	175 to 180°
Square Shoulder		
4 to 6 lbs.	30 to 35	175 to 180°

every 15 minutes with Mint Glaze (below). Serve any remaining glaze with roast.

Roasts are easier to carve if allowed to "set" 15 to 20 minutes after removing from oven. Since meat continues to cook after removal from oven, if roast is to set, it should be removed from oven when thermometer registers 5 to 10° lower than the desired doneness.

Mint Glaze

Heat ½ jar (10-ounce size) mint-flavored jelly, 1 clove garlic, crushed, and 2 teaspoons water, stirring constantly, until jelly is melted.

BULGUR PILAF

   1 tablespoon finely chopped onion
   1 tablespoon chopped green pepper
   1 tablespoon butter or margarine
   ⅔ cup hot water
   ½ teaspoon instant chicken bouillon
   ⅓ cup bulgur wheat
   1 can (2 ounces) sliced mushrooms, drained
   ¼ teaspoon salt
     Dash pepper

In 8-inch skillet, cook and stir onion and green pepper in butter until onion is tender. Stir in remaining ingredients. Heat to boiling. Reduce heat; cover and simmer 10 minutes. *2 servings.*

GOURMET PEARS

1 egg yolk*
3 tablespoons dairy sour cream
3 tablespoons granulated sugar
1 tablespoon rum, brandy or sherry
1 can (8 ounces) pears, drained
2 tablespoons brown sugar

In small saucepan, mix egg yolk, sour cream and granulated sugar. Cook, stirring constantly, until sauce is thickened, about 3 minutes. Cool. (Store in refrigerator if not using immediately.)

Stir rum into sour cream sauce. Place pears in 2 ungreased 6-ounce baking dishes or one 1¾-cup casserole. Pour sauce onto pears; sprinkle with brown sugar. Set oven control at broil and/or 550°. Broil with tops 6 to 8 inches from heat until brown sugar melts, 3 to 4 minutes. Serve hot or chilled. *2 servings.*

* What about the egg white? Store in covered small container in refrigerator up to 3 days. Can be used for Individual Brownie Alaskas (page 6). Or add to whole eggs when preparing scrambled eggs.

Look-ahead lamb still has that international air. When the next time comes, go East or West—Chinese or American.

CHOPPED LAMB SANDWICH FILLING

½   cup chopped cooked lamb
2   tablespoons mayonnaise or salad dressing
3   tablespoons finely chopped celery
1½   teaspoons finely chopped onion
1   teaspoon prepared mustard

Mix all ingredients. Good on rye bread. *¾ cup (enough for 2 sandwiches).*

CHINESE LAMB SUEY

2   tablespoons butter or margarine
1½   cups cooked lamb strips, 2x¼x¼ inch
1   small onion, sliced and separated into rings
½   can (8-ounce size) water chestnuts, sliced
¾   cup water
1   tablespoon soy sauce
1   tablespoon cornstarch
¾   teaspoon instant beef bouillon
½   teaspoon salt
1   package (6 ounces) frozen pea pods
Hot cooked rice or chow mein noodles

Melt butter in 8-inch skillet; cook and stir meat and onion over medium heat until meat is brown and onion is tender. Add remaining ingredients except pea pods and rice. Heat to boiling, stirring occasionally. Add pea pods; cover and simmer 5 minutes. Serve on rice. *2 servings.*

SHEPHERDS' PIE

Instant mashed potatoes (enough for 4 servings)
1 tablespoon parsley flakes or snipped parsley
1 envelope (about 1 ounce) gravy mix
1 cup cubed cooked lamb, beef or veal
2 tablespoons chopped onion
1 cup cooked vegetables (peas, carrots, corn,
  green beans)
¼ teaspoon salt

Heat oven to 350°. Prepare potatoes as directed on package except—stir in parsley flakes. Prepare gravy mix as directed.

In ungreased 1-quart casserole, mix gravy and remaining ingredients. Mound potatoes on meat mixture. Bake uncovered until potatoes are light brown, 25 to 30 minutes. *2 servings.*

LAMB WITH DILL SAUCE

1 tablespoon butter or margarine
1 tablespoon flour
⅓ cup water
½ teaspoon instant chicken bouillon
2 tablespoon vinegar
½ teaspoon dill weed
  Salt and pepper
2 to 4 slices cooked lamb, ⅜ inch thick

Melt butter in small saucepan. Stir in flour. Cook over low heat, stirring until mixture is smooth and bubbly. Stir in water and bouillon. Heat to boiling, stirring constantly. Boil and stir 1 minute. Stir in vinegar and dill weed. Season with salt and pepper. Add meat and heat. Garnish with snipped parsley if desired. *2 servings.*

Baked Ham
Pecan Sweet Potatoes
Cauliflower with Nutmeg Butter
Molded Lime-Pineapple Salad
Brown and Serve Rolls
Mocha Parfaits (page 31)

What a feast—a real old-time baked ham dinner. And no, you don't have to keep on eating it day after day. Just cut into portions called for by the recipes on pages 143–145, wrap for freezing (be sure to label) and use within 3 to 4 weeks.

Idea: A tiny canned ham can be a lifesaver-for-two (especially the 1½-pound size). Try to keep one on your "emergency" shelf. But watch it—some need refrigeration, some don't. Look to the label.

BAKED HAM

Place ham fat side up on rack in shallow roasting pan. Insert meat thermometer so tip is in center of thickest part of meat and does not touch bone or rest in fat.

Roast uncovered in 325° oven until done (see Timetable at right), using thermometer reading as final guide. Ham is easier to carve if allowed to "set" 15 to 20 minutes after removing from oven. Since meat continues to cook after removal from oven, if ham is to set, it should be removed when thermometer registers 5° lower than desired doneness.

TIMETABLE

Cut	Approximate Cooking Time (Minutes per Lb.)	Meat Thermometer Reading
Ham (fully cooked)		
Half		
5 to 7 lbs.	18 to 24	140°
Shank or rump (butt) portion		
3 to 4 lbs.	18 to 24	140°
Ham (cook before eating)		
Half		
5 to 7 lbs.	22 to 25	160°
Shank or rump (butt) portion		
3 to 4 lbs.	35 to 40	160°
Smoked Shoulder Roll		
2 to 4 lbs.	35 to 40	170°

PECAN SWEET POTATOES

Heat oven to 325°. Place 1 can (8 ounces) sweet potatoes in syrup, drained, in ungreased 1¾-cup casserole. Sprinkle with 3 tablespoons brown sugar and dot with 1 tablespoon butter. Bake uncovered until hot and bubbly, 25 to 30 minutes. Sprinkle with 1 to 2 tablespoons broken pecans. *2 servings.*

CAULIFLOWER WITH NUTMEG BUTTER

Heat 1 inch salted water (½ teaspoon salt to 1 cup water) to boiling. Add 1 small cauliflower. Cover; heat to boiling. Cook until tender, 12 to 15 minutes. Drain; turn into serving dish. Dot with butter and sprinkle with nutmeg. *2 servings*.

MOLDED LIME-PINEAPPLE SALAD

> 1 **cup boiling water**
> 1 **package (3 ounces) lime-flavored gelatin**
> 1 **can (8¾ ounces) crushed pineapple, drained**
>   **(reserve syrup)**
>   **Lettuce**
>   **Mayonnaise**

Pour boiling water on gelatin in bowl; stir until gelatin is dissolved. Add enough water to reserved pineapple syrup to measure 1 cup; stir into gelatin. Chill until thickened but not set.

Stir in pineapple. Pour into 4 to 6 individual molds or one 4-cup mold. Chill until firm. Place 2 servings on lettuce and top each with mayonnaise. Serve remaining gelatin topped with whipped cream as a dessert the next day. *2 servings—and 2 to 4 for another day*.

Four impressive planned-overs from That Ham. Note especially the unique Ham 'n Cheese Supper Bread. Be sure to serve it warm, with soup and a jumbo salad.

HAM 'N CHEESE SUPPER BREAD

- 1 cup buttermilk baking mix
- ½ cup chopped cooked ham
- 2 tablespoons instant minced onion
- 1 egg
- ⅓ cup milk
- 1 tablespoon salad oil
- ¼ teaspoon prepared mustard
- 1 cup shredded Cheddar cheese (about 4 ounces)
- 1 tablespoon sesame seed

Heat oven to 350°. Grease 1-quart casserole. Mix baking mix, ham, onion, egg, milk, oil, mustard and ⅔ cup of the cheese. Spread in casserole. Sprinkle remaining cheese and the sesame seed on top. Bake until top is golden brown, 30 to 35 minutes. Serve warm. *2 servings.*

Note: Wrap leftover bread in aluminum foil and refrigerate or freeze. Heat in wrapping in 400° oven until warm, about 10 minutes (if frozen, 30 to 35 minutes).

EGGS BENEDICT

> 2 eggs
> 1 envelope (1¼ ounces) hollandaise sauce mix
> 2 thin slices cooked ham
> 1 English muffin, split and toasted

Heat water (1½ to 2 inches) in saucepan or skillet to boiling; reduce heat to simmer. Break eggs, 1 at a time, into custard cup or saucer; holding cup or saucer close to surface of water, slip egg into water. Cook until eggs reach desired doneness, 3 to 5 minutes.

While eggs cook, prepare hollandaise sauce as directed on package. Place slice of ham on each muffin half, then top with an egg and half the hollandaise sauce. *2 servings*.

SCALLOPED POTATOES WITH HAM

Heat oven to 400°. Measure contents of 1 package (5.5 ounces) scalloped potatoes; divide in half (approximately 1 cup potato slices and 3 tablespoons sauce mix).* Place potato slices in ungreased 1-quart casserole; sprinkle half the sauce mix on potato slices. Add 1 cup cut-up cooked ham and stir in half the amounts of water and milk called for on package. Bake uncovered until potatoes are tender and golden brown, 25 to 30 minutes. *2 servings*.

*To store remaining mix, close package securely and use within 2 weeks. Make Quick Scalloped Potatoes (page 59) and serve with pork chops, ham, frankfurters or hamburgers.

CHILI-BEAN SKILLET

- 1 cup cubed cooked ham
- ½ cup sliced celery
- ¼ cup chopped onion
- ¼ cup chopped green pepper
  Dash instant minced garlic
- ½ teaspoon salt
- 2 tablespoons salad oil
- 1 can (8 ounces) pork and beans
- 1 can (8 ounces) lima beans
- ⅓ cup chili sauce

In 8-inch skillet, cook and stir ham, celery, onion, green pepper, garlic and salt in oil until onion is tender. Drain off fat. Stir in pork and beans, lima beans (with liquid) and chili sauce; simmer uncovered until hot, about 10 minutes. *2 servings*.

**Roast Beef with Oven-browned Potatoes
Sautéed Cherry Tomatoes
Marinated Asparagus Spears
Lemon Sherbet with
Raspberry-Currant Sauce (page 122)**

*A lordly beef roast. Who can resist it? Figure on about
½ pound per serving—less for boneless, a little more
for bone-in. If leftovers are minimal, you can refrigerate promptly and use within one or two days. Choose
the rolled rump if you're watching the budget. Another
time try the boneless rib for a fabulous feast for two.*

ROAST BEEF WITH
OVEN-BROWNED POTATOES

Place roast fat side up on rack in shallow roasting pan.
Season with salt and pepper before, during or after
roasting (salt goes into roast only ¼ to ½ inch). Insert
meat thermometer to tip is in center of thickest part of
meat and does not rest in fat.

Roast uncovered in 325° oven until done (see Timetable at right), using thermometer reading as final
guide. About 1½ hours before roast is done, pare 2
medium baking potatoes. If you wish, make thin crosswise cuts almost through potatoes. Heat 1 inch salted
water (½ teaspoon salt to 1 cup water) to boiling. Add
potatoes. Cover and heat to boiling; cook 10 minutes.
Drain.

TIMETABLE

Cut	Approximate Cooking Time (Minutes per Lb.)	Meat Thermometer Reading
Boneless Rib	32	140° (rare)
5 to 7 lbs.	38	160° (medium)
	48	170° (well)
Rib Eye (Delmonico)*	18 to 20	140° (rare)
	20 to 22	160° (medium)
4 to 5 lbs.	22 to 24	170° (well)
Tip Roast (high quality)	35 to 40	150 to 170°
3½ to 4 lbs.		
Rolled Rump (high quality)	25 to 30	150 to 170°
4 to 5 lbs.		

*Roast at 350°.

Place potatoes in meat drippings in roasting pan; turn each potato to coat with fat. Or brush potatoes with melted butter or margarine and place on rack with meat. Turning potatoes once, bake until tender and golden brown, 1¼ to 1½ hours. Season with salt and pepper.

Roasts are easier to carve if allowed to "set" 15 to 20 minutes after removing from oven. Since meat continues to cook after removal from oven, if roast is to set, it should be removed from oven when thermometer registers 5° lower than the desired doneness. Serve with meat juices or Pan Gravy (page 53). *2 servings*.

SAUTÉED CHERRY TOMATOES

Remove stem ends from ½ pint cherry tomatoes. Prick each tomato several times. Melt 1 tablespoon butter or margarine in 8-inch skillet. Cook and stir tomatoes in butter over medium heat until heated through, about 3 minutes. For a garnish, sprinkle snipped chives on top. *2 servings*.

MARINATED ASPARAGUS SPEARS

  1 **package (10 ounces) frozen asparagus spears**
  ½ **cup Italian dressing**
   Lettuce leaves
   Pimiento strips

Cook asparagus spears as directed on package. Drain and turn into bowl. Pour dressing on hot asparagus; cover and refrigerate 2 to 3 hours. Serve spears on lettuce leaves and garnish with pimiento strips. *2 servings*.

Now revel in your beef leftovers! Savor Beef
Rolls in Wine, a recipe you may well want to
double to share with a pair of discriminating
friends. Enjoy a superb main-dish salad. And
by all means, get familiar with the quick skillet dish—it lets you shine even when you've
plain run out of time!

HERBED BEEF AND ONIONS

    2 tablespoons butter or margarine
    1 medium onion, sliced and separated into rings
    4 slices cooked roast beef
    2 teaspoons vinegar
    1 tablespoon butter or margarine, softened
    ⅛ teaspoon thyme, tarragon or marjoram leaves

Melt 2 tablespoons butter in 8-inch skillet; cook and
stir onion until tender, about 5 minutes. Remove onion
from skillet and keep warm.

    Add meat to skillet; brown quickly on both sides and
sprinkle with vinegar. Mix 1 tablespoon butter and the
thyme leaves. Arrange meat and onions on dinner
plates; top meat with seasoned butter. *2 servings*.

BEEF ROLLS IN WINE

1   **can (2 ounces) mushroom stems and pieces,
    drained and chopped**
2   **tablespoons chopped onion**
4   **thin slices cooked roast beef**
1   **tablespoon salad oil**
1   **can (16 ounces) whole carrots, drained
    (reserve liquid)**
3   **tablespoons red wine**
3   **tablespoons gravy mix (dry)**
¼   **teaspoon salt**
¼   **teaspoon pepper**
    Dash thyme
    Snipped parsley

Mix mushrooms and onion; place ¼ of mixture on
center of each beef slice. Roll up and fasten with
wooden picks. Heat oil in 8-inch skillet; brown rolls.
Add enough water to reserved carrot liquid to measure
1 cup. Stir carrot liquid, wine, gravy mix, salt, pepper
and thyme into skillet. Heat to boiling. Reduce heat;
cover and simmer 10 minutes. Add carrots; simmer
until hot, about 10 minutes. Garnish with parsley. *2
servings*.

CHILI CHEF'S SALAD

- ½ cup julienne strips cooked meat (beef, ham, tongue, luncheon meat)
- ½ cup julienne strips cooked chicken or turkey
- ½ cup julienne strips Swiss cheese
- ¼ cup chopped green onion
- ¼ cup sliced celery
- 8 cups bite-size pieces lettuce (iceberg and/or romaine)
- ⅓ cup mayonnaise or salad dressing
- ⅓ cup chili sauce
  Ripe olives
- 1 hard-cooked egg, cut into wedges

Reserve few strips of meat, chicken and cheese for garnish. In large bowl, toss remaining meat, chicken, cheese, the onion, celery and lettuce. Mix mayonnaise and chili sauce; pour on salad and toss. Garnish with reserved meat, chicken and cheese, the olives and egg wedges. *2 generous servings*.

Celery Victor
Roast Turkey
Giblet Gravy
Cranberry Sauce
Mashed Potatoes
Broccoli with Lemon Butter
Hot Cloverleaf Rolls
Pumpkin Custards

CELERY VICTOR

1 bunch celery
1 cup water
1 teaspoon instant beef bouillon
⅓ cup Italian dressing

Trim off root end of celery bunch but do not separate stalks. Remove leaves and coarse outer stalks; reserve some leaves for garnish. Cut celery bunch crosswise so bottom section is 3 inches long. (Refrigerate top section for future use.) Cut bottom section crosswise in half; tie halves with string.

In small saucepan, heat water and bouillon to boiling. Add celery halves; heat to boiling. Cover and cook until tender, about 15 minutes. Drain. Place celery halves in shallow 1-quart casserole; pour dressing on halves. Refrigerate 3 hours, spooning dressing on halves 2 or 3 times. Place celery half on each salad plate; remove string. Garnish with pimiento strips and celery leaves. *2 servings*.

ROAST TURKEY

Choose a 4- to 8-pound fryer-roaster turkey. If turkey is frozen, thaw as directed on package. Wash turkey and pat dry.

If turkey is to be stuffed, stuff just before roasting. Use ½ package (7-ounce size) herbed stuffing and half the amounts of butter and water called for on package; prepare as directed. Fill wishbone area with stuffing first; fasten neck skin to back with skewer. Fold wings across back with tips touching. Fill body cavity lightly. (Do not pack—stuffing will expand while cooking.) Tuck drumsticks under band of skin at tail or tie together with heavy string, then tie to tail.

Place turkey breast side up on rack in shallow roasting pan. Brush with butter, salad oil or shortening. Insert meat thermometer so tip is in thickest part of inside thigh muscle or thickest part of breast meat and does not touch bone.

Roast uncovered in 325° oven, brushing occasionally with butter or pan drippings, until tender, 2½ to 3½ hours. If turkey is browning too quickly, cover loosely with aluminum foil. Meat thermometer should register 180 to 185°. Or test for doneness by pressing thickest part of the drumstick between protected fingers—if done, the meat should feel very soft. Or move drumstick up and down—if done, the joint should give readily or break.

When turkey is done, remove from oven and allow to stand about 20 minutes for easiest carving. Serve with Giblet Gravy (on page 154) if you wish.

Remove every bit of stuffing from turkey as soon as possible after serving. Cool stuffing, meat and any gravy promptly; refrigerate separately. Use gravy or stuffing within 1 or 2 days; heat them thoroughly before serving. Serve cooked turkey meat within 2 or 3 days after roasting. If frozen, it can be kept up to 1 month.

GIBLET GRAVY

While turkey is roasting, cook giblets: In small saucepan, heat gizzard, heart, neck, ¼ teaspoon salt, 2 peppercorns, 1 bay leaf and enough water to cover to boiling. Reduce heat; cover and simmer until gizzard is fork tender, about 1 hour. Add liver during last 15 minutes of cooking. Remove meat from neck; finely chop giblets and reserve broth.

Pour drippings from roasting pan into bowl, leaving brown particles in pan. Return 1 tablespoon drippings to pan. Mix in 1 tablespoon flour. Cook over low heat, stirring until mixture is smooth and bubbly. Remove from heat. Stir in ½ cup of the reserved broth. Heat to boiling, stirring constantly. Boil and stir 1 minute. Stir in giblets and heat through. *About ¾ cup.*

MASHED POTATOES

   3 **medium potatoes (about 1 pound)**
      About ¼ cup milk
   2 **tablespoons soft butter or margarine**
   ¼ **teaspoon salt**
      Dash pepper

Pare potatoes. Heat 1 inch salted water (½ teaspoon salt to 1 cup water) to boiling. Add potatoes. Cover and heat to boiling; cook until tender—30 to 35 minutes for whole potatoes, 20 to 25 minutes for cut. Drain. Gently shake pan over low heat to dry potatoes.

Mash potatoes until no lumps remain. Add milk in small amounts, beating after each addition. (Amount of milk needed to make potatoes smooth and fluffy depends on kind of potatoes.) Add butter, salt and pepper; beat until potatoes are light and fluffy. Dot with butter or sprinkle paprika or snipped parsley on top. *2 servings*.

PUMPKIN CUSTARDS

½ can (16-ounce size) pumpkin pie mix*
1 egg, slightly beaten
½ cup milk
   Streusel Topping (below)

Heat oven to 325°. Mix pie mix, egg and milk until smooth. Pour into 2 ungreased 10-ounce custard cups. Sprinkle Streusel Topping on top. Place cups in baking pan, 9x9x2 inches; pour very hot water into pan to within ½ inch of tops of cups.

Bake until knife inserted halfway between center and edge comes out clean, about 1 hour. Remove cups from water. Serve warm or chilled. *2 servings*.

Streusel Topping

¼ cup brown sugar (packed)
2 tablespoons flour
2 tablespoons chopped pecans
¼ teaspoon cinnamon
2 tablespoons soft butter or margarine

Mix all ingredients with fork until crumbly.

*Leftover pumpkin pie mix? Use in Frosty Pumpkin Custard (page 99).

Look what you can do for a turkey encore:
salads, sandwiches, a quick one-dish dinner.
Take off from there. Have fun!

BACON-TURKEY CLUB SALAD

    6 cups bite-size pieces lettuce
    4 or 5 slices bacon, crisply fried and crumbled
    1 medium tomato, cut into wedges
 1½ cups cut-up cooked turkey
    1 hard-cooked egg, sliced
       Barbecue Dressing (below)

Toss lettuce, bacon, tomato and turkey in bowl. Garnish with egg slices. Serve with dressing. *2 servings*.

Barbecue Dressing

 ¼ cup mayonnaise or salad dressing
    2 tablespoons barbecue sauce
    2 teaspoons instant minced onion
    2 teaspoons lemon juice
 ¼ teaspoon salt
 ⅛ teaspoon pepper

Mix all ingredients. *About ⅓ cup*.

BROILED TURKEY AND CHEESE SANDWICHES

- **1 package (10 ounces) frozen asparagus spears or broccoli spears**
- **2 tablespoons deviled ham, if desired**
- **2 slices toast, buttered**
  Sliced cooked turkey
- **2 slices process American cheese**

Cook asparagus spears as directed on package. Drain. Spread 1 tablespoon ham on each slice toast. Top with turkey slices, half the asparagus spears and a cheese slice.

Set oven control at broil and/or 550°. Broil sandwiches with tops 6 inches from heat just until cheese is bubbly, about 1 minute. Watch carefully! *2 servings.*

HOT TURKEY SUPPER SALAD

- **1 cup cut-up cooked turkey**
- **1 cup thinly sliced celery**
- **½ cup croutons**
- **½ cup mayonnaise**
- **¼ cup diced roasted almonds**
- **1 tablespoon lemon juice**
- **1 teaspoon onion salt**
- **¼ cup shredded Cheddar cheese**
- **½ cup croutons or crushed potato chips**

Heat oven to 350°. Mix all ingredients except cheese and ½ cup croutons. Divide between 2 ungreased 1½-cup casseroles. Sprinkle cheese and ½ cup croutons on tops. Bake 20 to 25 minutes. *2 servings.*

TURKEY CREOLE

   1 **small onion, thinly sliced**
   ½ **small green pepper, cut into narrow strips**
   ¼ **cup thinly sliced celery**
   1 **tablespoon salad oil**
   1 **can (8 ounces) stewed tomatoes**
   1 **can (8 ounces) tomato sauce**
   1 to 1½ **teaspoons chili powder**
   ¼ **teaspoon salt**
1½ **cups cut-up cooked turkey**
      Hot cooked rice or spaghetti

In 8-inch skillet, cook and stir onion, green pepper and
celery in oil until vegetables are tender, about 5 minutes. Stir in tomatoes, tomato sauce, chili powder and
salt; simmer uncovered 10 minutes. Stir in turkey;
cover and simmer until turkey is hot, about 5 minutes.
Serve on rice. *2 servings*.

TWO IS COMPANY

Memory-making dinners that say,
"Tonight is special"

Herb-roasted Chicken
Parsleyed Mixed Vegetables
Hot Crusty Rolls
Crêpes Suzette

HERB-ROASTED CHICKEN

2½- to 3-pound broiler-fryer chicken
 ¼ cup butter or margarine, melted
 ¼ teaspoon rosemary
 ¼ teaspoon thyme
 ¼ teaspoon marjoram
    Parsleyed Mixed Vegetables (on page 160)
    Parsley

Heat oven to 375°. Rub cavity of chicken with salt if desired. Place chicken breast side up on rack in roasting pan. Mix butter, rosemary, thyme and marjoram; brush half the herb-butter mixture on chicken. Roast uncovered until done, 1¼ to 1¾ hours, brushing chicken with remaining herb-butter mixture several times. If chicken is browning too quickly, cover loosely with aluminum foil. Chicken is done when drumstick meat feels very soft when pressed. Place chicken on heated platter; surround with vegetables and garnish with parsley. *2 servings*.

PARSLEYED MIXED VEGETABLES

    4 small or medium potatoes, pared
    2 medium carrots, cut lengthwise into halves
    2 small onions
    ½ teaspoon seasoned salt
    ¼ cup water or chicken broth
    2 small zucchini, cut lengthwise into quarters
    ½ teaspoon seasoned salt
       Snipped parsley

Heat oven to 375°. If using medium potatoes, cut each
in half. Combine all ingredients except zucchini, ½
teaspoon seasoned salt and the parsley in ungreased
1-quart casserole. Cover and bake 50 minutes. Add
zucchini and salt; bake until vegetables are done, about
10 minutes. Arrange vegetables on platter; spoon on
some liquid and sprinkle with parsley. *2 servings*.

CRÊPES SUZETTE

       Crêpes (at right)
    ¼ cup butter or margarine
    ¼ teaspoon grated orange peel
    ¼ cup orange juice
    1 tablespoon sugar
    2 tablespoons orange-flavored liqueur or
       2 tablespoons brandy

Prepare Crêpes. In 8-inch skillet, heat butter, orange
peel, orange juice and sugar to boiling, stirring occasionally. Boil and stir 1 minute. Reduce heat. Fold
crêpes into fourths; place in hot orange sauce, turning
crêpes once.
    To flame, heat orange-flavored liqueur just until
warm in long-handled ladle or small pan. Ignite and

pour flaming over crêpes in skillet. Place 2 crêpes on each dessert plate; spoon sauce on crêpes. *2 servings*.

Crêpes

½ **cup all-purpose flour**
1 **teaspoon sugar**
¼ **teaspoon baking powder**
¼ **teaspoon salt**
⅔ **cup milk**
1 **egg**
¼ **teaspoon vanilla**
2 **teaspoons butter or margarine, melted**

Beat all ingredients with rotary beater until smooth. For each crêpe, lightly butter 8-inch skillet; heat over medium heat until butter is bubbly. Pour scant ¼ cup batter into skillet; immediately rotate pan until batter covers bottom. Cook until light brown; turn and brown other side. Stack crêpes so first-baked side is down. Cool, keeping crêpes covered to prevent them from drying out. *4 to 6 crêpes*.

Note: As soon as you pour the crêpe batter into the skillet, quickly rotate the pan so that the batter covers the bottom evenly.

The tissue-thin crêpe can be lifted easily. Check the color of the bottom to see if it's time to turn it—it should be light brown.

Dim the lights, then bring out the crêpes in their orange sauce and flame them at the table for a triumphant finale to your dinner.

Lamb Shish Kabobs
Parsleyed Rice
Greek Salad
Sesame Hard Rolls
Raspberry Crème
Almond Cookies

LAMB SHISH KABOBS

¾ pound boneless lamb shoulder, cut into 1-inch cubes
¼ cup Caesar dressing or French dressing
1 can (8 ounces) whole onions, drained
About 8 pineapple chunks
Green pepper pieces (½ pepper)
Red pepper pieces (½ pepper)
Parsleyed Rice (below)

Place meat in glass bowl; pour dressing on meat. Cover and refrigerate at least 8 hours.

Remove meat from marinade; reserve marinade. Alternate meat cubes, onions, pineapple chunks and green and red pepper pieces on each of 4 skewers. Set oven control at broil and/or 550°. Place skewers on rack in broiler pan. Brush some of the reserved marinade on kabobs. Broil with tops 4 to 5 inches from heat until meat is brown, about 6 minutes. Turn; brush remaining marinade on kabobs. Broil until done, about 5 minutes. Serve kabobs on Parsleyed Rice. *2 servings*.

PARSLEYED RICE

Cook instant rice as directed on package for 2 servings. Stir in 1 tablespoon snipped parsley.

GREEK SALAD

> 2 small heads Bibb lettuce
> 1 medium tomato, cut into wedges
> 6 pitted ripe olives
> ⅛ teaspoon oregano
> 1 tablespoon crumbled feta cheese or blue cheese
>   Lemon-Oil Dressing (below)
>   Lemon wedges

Place 1 head Bibb lettuce on each salad plate. Arrange tomato wedges and olives between leaves. Sprinkle oregano and cheese on salads; drizzle with dressing. Garnish salads with lemon wedges. *2 servings*.

Lemon-Oil Dressing

> ¼ cup olive oil or salad oil
> 1 tablespoon lemon juice
> ⅛ teaspoon salt
>   Dash pepper

Shake all ingredients in tightly covered jar. *About ¼ cup*.

RASPBERRY CRÈME

Mix 1 carton (8 ounces) raspberry yogurt and ½ cup frozen whipped topping (thawed). Divide between dessert dishes. Top with a dollop of whipped topping and garnish with mint leaves. *2 servings*.

Coq au Vin
Tossed Romaine Salad
Crusty French Bread
Pots de Crème au Chocolat

COQ AU VIN

    3 slices bacon
    ¼ cup all-purpose flour
    ½ teaspoon salt
    ⅛ teaspoon pepper
    1½ pounds chicken pieces (legs, thighs, breasts)
    ¼ pound fresh mushrooms, sliced
    2 small onions, cut into halves
    2 carrots, cut diagonally into 2-inch pieces
    1 teaspoon instant chicken bouillon or 1 chicken
       bouillon cube
    ½ teaspoon Italian herb seasoning or ⅛ teaspoon each
       thyme, basil, marjoram and sage
    ¾ cup water
    ½ cup red Burgundy
       Snipped parsley

In Dutch oven or 3-quart saucepan, fry bacon until
crisp; remove and drain. Mix flour, salt and pepper in
plastic or paper bag. Shake chicken, 2 or 3 pieces at a
time, in bag until coated. Brown chicken in bacon fat;
remove to warm platter.

Cook and stir mushrooms and onion in Dutch oven
until onion is tender. Drain off fat. Place chicken in
Dutch oven; crumble bacon on chicken and add re-

maining ingredients except parsley. Heat to boiling.
Reduce heat; cover and simmer until thickest chicken
pieces are tender, about 30 minutes. Sprinkle parsley
on top. *2 servings*.

TOSSED ROMAINE SALAD

    3 cups bite-size pieces romaine (1 small head)
    4 or 5 radishes, sliced
    2 tablespoons salad oil
    1 tablespoon wine, tarragon or cider vinegar
    1 small clove garlic, crushed, or ⅛ teaspoon garlic
      powder
    ¼ teaspoon salt
      Dash pepper

Combine romaine and radish slices in bowl. Mix remaining ingredients; pour onto vegetables and toss. *2
servings*.

POTS DE CRÈME AU CHOCOLAT

    ½ bar (4-ounce size) sweet cooking chocolate
    1 tablespoon sugar
    ⅓ cup light cream (20%) or half-and-half
    1 egg yolk, slightly beaten
    ¼ teaspoon vanilla

In small saucepan, cook chocolate, sugar and cream
over medium heat, stirring constantly, until chocolate
is melted and mixture is smooth. Remove from heat;
beat into egg yolk. Stir in vanilla. Pour into pots de
crème cups, demitasse cups or other small dessert
dishes. Chill. If you like, serve with whipped cream
and garnish with mint leaf. *2 servings*.

Sweet-and-Sour Pork
Fluffy White Rice
Chinese Pea Pods
Carrot Sticks
Cucumber Sticks
Melon Boats with Sherbet

SWEET-AND-SOUR PORK

Salad oil
Sweet-and-Sour Sauce (at right)
½ cup all-purpose flour
¼ cup cornstarch
1 teaspoon salt
¼ teaspoon monosodium glutamate
½ teaspoon baking powder
½ cup water
1 teaspoon salad oil
½ pound pork tenderloin, cut into ¼-inch slices
1 medium green pepper, cut into 1-inch pieces
1 small onion, cut into 1-inch pieces
1½ cups hot cooked rice

Pour oil into electric skillet or large saucepan to depth
of 1 to 1½ inches. Heat to 375°, or until 1-inch bread
cube browns in 1 minute. While oil heats, prepare
Sweet-and-Sour Sauce.

In small bowl, beat flour, cornstarch, salt, monosodium glutamate, baking powder, water and 1 teaspoon oil with rotary beater until smooth. Dip meat
into batter with tongs; fry in hot oil, turning once, until
golden brown, 6 to 8 minutes. Drain; keep warm.

Stir green pepper and onion into Sweet-and-Sour

Sauce. Cover and simmer until vegetables are crisp-tender, about 5 minutes. Serve meat and sauce on rice.
2 servings.

Sweet-and-Sour Sauce

- ¼ **cup brown sugar (packed)**
- 2 **tablespoons cornstarch**
- 1 **can (8¼ ounces) pineapple chunks, drained (reserve syrup)**
- ¼ **cup vinegar**
- 2 **tablespoons catsup**

In 2-quart saucepan, mix sugar and cornstarch. Add enough water to reserved pineapple syrup to measure 1 cup. Stir syrup mixture, vinegar and catsup into cornstarch mixture. Cook, stirring constantly, until mixture thickens and boils. Stir in pineapple. Keep warm over very low heat.

SOMETHING TO KNOW ABOUT ...

Use tongs to dip each piece of pork into the batter; fry each piece as you've battered it. The pork will be easier to slice thin if it's partially frozen.

MELON BOATS WITH SHERBET

Top wedges of chilled honeydew melon or cantaloupe with scoops of lemon or lime sherbet.

Note: Melon out of season? Use 1 package (12 ounces) frozen melon balls, partially thawed, instead.

Oriental Fondue
Fluffy White Rice
Kumquats
Almond Cookies
Tea

ORIENTAL FONDUE

Choose one to three of the following meats and sea-foods to total ¾ pound:

> Pork tenderloin, cut into ⅛-inch slices
> Chicken breasts, boned and cut across grain into
> bite-size slices (about ¼ inch thick)
> Frozen scallops, thawed and cut into ¾-inch pieces
> Cleaned raw shrimp, fresh or frozen*

Choose three or four of the following vegetables:

> ¼ cauliflower, separated into flowerets
> ¼ pound broccoli, separated into flowerets
> ½ package (10-ounce size) frozen Chinese pea pods
> 2 medium carrots, cut diagonally into ⅛-inch slices
> ¼ pound fresh mushrooms, thinly sliced
> 1 bunch green onions (about 6), cut into
> ½-inch lengths

And have ready:

> 8 cups chicken broth**
> 1½ cups hot cooked rice
> Choice of dipping sauce (on pages 169 and 170)

Arrange meat, seafood and vegetables on tray or platter; garnish with parsley. Cover and refrigerate until serving time.

Pour chicken broth into 10-inch electric skillet, metal fondue pot or chafing dish until about ⅔ full (add any remaining chicken broth as needed); heat to simmering. Divide rice between 2 small bowls. Serve dipping sauces in small bowls.

Each person uses chopsticks or fondue forks to place an assortment of meat and vegetables (2 or 3 pieces at a time) in broth. Cook foods until done, 2 to 4 minutes; transfer to dinner plate and dip into a sauce. After the main course, ladle broth on remaining rice in bowls and eat as soup. *2 servings*.

Note: Meat will slice easier if partially frozen.

*Rinse frozen shrimp under running cold water to remove ice glaze.

**4 cans (13¾ ounces each) chicken broth and 1 cup water or 3 cans (10½ ounces each) condensed chicken broth, diluted as directed.

Lemon-Soy Sauce

  ¼ cup lemon juice
  ¼ cup soy sauce
   2 tablespoons sweet sake (for cooking) or sherry

Mix all ingredients. *About ½ cup*.

Sweet-and-Sour Sauce

2 tablespoons brown sugar
1 teaspoon cornstarch
2 tablespoons cider vinegar
⅓ cup pineapple juice
1 tablespoon catsup

Mix all ingredients in small saucepan. Cook over medium-high heat, stirring constantly, until mixture thickens and boils. Boil and stir 1 minute. *About ½ cup.*

Plum Sauce

¼ cup chili sauce
¼ cup plum jam or grape jelly
¼ teaspoon hot sauce

Mix all ingredients. *About ½ cup.*

Hot Mustard Sauce

3 tablespoons dry mustard
2 tablespoons water

Mix ingredients. *About ¼ cup.*

Roast Cornish Hens
Wild Rice with Mushrooms and Almonds
Artichokes with Lemon Butter
Crescent Rolls
Pots de Crème au Chocolat (page 165)

ROAST CORNISH HENS

 2 **Rock Cornish hens (about 1 pound each)**
   Salt
 ¼ **cup soft butter or margarine**
 ¼ **teaspoon red pepper sauce or ½ teaspoon thyme,**
   marjoram or tarragon leaves
   Preserved kumquats
   Watercress

Thaw hens if frozen. Heat oven to 350°. Rub cavities
of hens with salt if desired. Place hens breast side up on
rack in shallow roasting pan. Mix butter and red pepper
sauce. Brush part of butter mixture on hens and sprinkle with salt. Roast uncovered until tender, about 1
hour, brushing hens 3 or 4 times with remaining butter
mixture. Garnish with preserved kumquats and watercress. *2 servings*.

WILD RICE WITH MUSHROOMS AND ALMONDS

  2 tablespoons butter or margarine
⅓ cup uncooked wild rice
  1 tablespoon slivered almonds
  1 tablespoon chopped onion
  1 can (2 ounces) mushroom stems and pieces
  1 cup chicken broth*

Melt butter in 8-inch skillet; cook and stir rice, almonds and onion until almonds are golden brown, about 10 minutes.

Heat oven to 350°. Stir mushrooms (with liquid) and chicken broth into skillet; heat to boiling. Pour rice mixture into ungreased 2½-cup casserole. Cover and bake until all liquid is absorbed and rice is tender, about 1 hour. *2 servings*.

*Chicken broth can be made by dissolving 1 chicken bouillon cube or 1 teaspoon instant chicken bouillon in 1 cup boiling water.

ARTICHOKES WITH LEMON BUTTER

1½ quarts water
  1 tablespoon lemon juice
½ teaspoon salt
  2 artichokes
    Lemon butter (at right)

In 3-quart saucepan, heat water, lemon juice and salt to boiling. Remove discolored leaves and the small leaves at base of each artichoke. Trim stem even with base of artichoke. Cut 1 inch off top and discard top.

Snip off points of remaining leaves with scissors. Tie each artichoke with string around side and from top to bottom to hold leaves in place. Place artichokes in saucepan; heat to boiling.

Reduce heat; cover and simmer until done, 30 to 40 minutes. (Artichokes are done when leaves pull off easily and bottom is tender when pierced with knife.) Remove artichokes with tongs or 2 large spoons; place upside down to drain. Remove string and serve upright. Serve hot with Lemon Butter. *2 servings*.

Lemon Butter

Heat ¼ cup butter or margarine, 1 teaspoon grated lemon peel and 2 tablespoons lemon juice over low heat until butter is melted. *About ⅓ cup*.

Note: To eat artichokes, pull off leaves one at a time. Dip base of leaf into Lemon Butter; turn leaf meaty side down and draw between teeth, scraping off meat portion. Discard leaf on plate. When all leaves have been removed, cut off the spiny choke and eat the smooth round bottom portion—a great delicacy.

Shrimp Curry
Condiments
Green Rice
Sesame Crackers
Baked Banana with Butter Pecan Ice Cream
Spiced Tea

SHRIMP CURRY

Condiments (below)
1 can (10½ ounces) condensed cream of shrimp soup
1 teaspoon parsley flakes
¾ teaspoon curry powder
1 tablespoon instant minced onion
12 ounces frozen cleaned raw shrimp*
Green Rice (at right)

Prepare Condiments. In medium saucepan, heat soup, parsley flakes, curry powder and onion to boiling, stirring occasionally. Stir in shrimp; heat to boiling. Reduce heat; cover and simmer until shrimp are done, about 10 minutes. Serve curry with Green Rice. *2 servings*.

*Rinse frozen shrimp under running cold water to remove ice glaze.

CONDIMENTS

Choose three to six of the following:

Diced tomatoes	Kumquats
Golden raisins	Chopped green pepper
Toasted shredded coconut	Grated orange peel
Chopped hard-cooked eggs	Grated lemon peel
Sweet pickle sticks	Salted diced almonds
Chutney	Currant jelly
	Peeled and sliced avocado

GREEN RICE

⅔ cup uncooked regular rice
½ cup chopped fresh spinach leaves
2 teaspoons instant minced onion
1 tablespoon butter or margarine
1 teaspoon salt
1⅓ cups boiling water

Heat oven to 350°. Mix all ingredients in ungreased 1-quart casserole. Cover and bake until liquid is absorbed and rice is tender, about 30 minutes. *2 servings*.

BAKED BANANA

Heat oven to 350°. Cut peeled large banana lengthwise in half. Place halves cut sides down in greased baking dish and brush with lemon juice.

Drizzle with 1 tablespoon butter or margarine, melted, and if desired, 2 teaspoons light rum or ¼ teaspoon rum flavoring. Sprinkle 1 teaspoon grated lemon peel and 2 teaspoons brown sugar on top. Bake uncovered 20 minutes. Serve warm with butter pecan ice cream or any favorite flavor. *2 servings*.

SPICED TEA

2 tea bags
3 whole cloves, broken into pieces
¼ teaspoon dried orange peel
⅛ teaspoon cinnamon
2 cups boiling water

In heated teapot or other heatproof container, place tea bags, cloves, orange peel and cinnamon. Pour boiling water into teapot. Cover and steep 3 to 5 minutes. Stir just before serving. *2 servings*.

Duckling à l'Orange
Barley Pilaf
Mushroom Green Beans or Spinach Soufflé
Tomato-Endive Toss
Mocha Ice-cream Puffs

DUCKLING À L'ORANGE

  4- to 5-pound duckling
  2 tablespoons butter or margarine
  2 tablespoons finely chopped onion
  ¼ teaspoon tarragon leaves
1½ tablespoons shredded orange peel
  ½ cup orange juice
  ¼ teaspoon salt
  ⅛ teaspoon dry mustard
  ¼ cup currant jelly
  2 tablespoons port or cranberry cocktail
  1 teaspoon cornstarch

Fasten neck skin of duckling with skewers. Lift wing tips up and over back for natural brace. Heat oven to 325°. Place duckling breast side up on rack in shallow roasting pan.

Melt butter in small saucepan. Cook and stir onion and tarragon leaves in butter until onion is tender. Add orange peel, orange juice, salt, mustard, jelly and port; cook and stir over medium heat until jelly is melted.

Measure orange sauce; reserve half the sauce to serve with duckling. Brush duckling with part of remaining orange sauce. Roast uncovered until done, about 2½ hours, pricking skin with fork and brushing occasionally with remaining orange sauce. If duckling is browning too quickly, cover loosely with aluminum foil. Duckling is done when drumstick meat feels very soft when pressed.

In small saucepan, mix reserved orange sauce and the cornstarch. Cook over medium heat, stirring constantly, until mixture boils. Boil and stir 1 minute. Serve sauce in small pitcher. Remove duckling to warm platter; garnish with watercress, orange twists, grapes or kumquats. *2 servings*.

SOMETHING TO KNOW ABOUT...

To serve the duckling after you've presented it at the table, cut it lengthwise in half. Keep close to the top of the wishbone and the center of the back. Then cut each half into 2 pieces. (Poultry shears work best for this, but you can also use kitchen shears or a sharp, sturdy knife.)

BARLEY PILAF

    1 tablespoon butter or margarine
    ⅓ cup uncooked barley
    1 tablespoon instant minced onion
    1 teaspoon instant chicken bouillon
    ¼ teaspoon celery salt
    ⅛ teaspoon pepper
    1 cup boiling water
    1 tablespoon snipped parsley

Heat oven to 325°. In ungreased 2½-cup casserole, mix all ingredients except parsley. Cover and bake until done, about 1 hour. Stir in parsley. *2 servings*.

MUSHROOM GREEN BEANS

1 can (2 ounces) mushroom stems and pieces, drained (reserve liquid)
½ package (10-ounce size) frozen French-style green beans
¼ teaspoon salt
1 teaspoon butter or margarine

Add enough water to reserved mushroom liquid to measure ¼ cup; pour into small saucepan. Add beans and salt. Cover and cook until tender, about 5 minutes. Drain. Stir in butter and mushrooms; heat through. *2 servings*.

SPINACH SOUFFLÉ

Heat oven to 325°. Remove frozen spinach soufflé (12-ounce size) from container. Cut into quarters. Place 2 quarters in each of 2 ungreased 10-ounce baking dishes, overlapping quarters if necessary. Bake until knife inserted in center comes out clean, 50 to 60 minutes. *2 servings*.

TOMATO-ENDIVE TOSS

3 cups bite-size pieces endive
2 tomatoes, cut into wedges
Oil-and-Vinegar Dressing (page 95)
Onion rings
Marinated artichoke hearts, if desired

Toss endive, tomatoes and the dressing. Garnish with onion rings and artichoke hearts. *2 servings*.

MOCHA ICE-CREAM PUFFS

- ½ **cup water**
- ¼ **cup butter or margarine**
- ½ **cup all-purpose flour**
- 2 **eggs**
   Coffee ice cream
- ¼ **cup chocolate syrup**
- 2 **teaspoons orange-flavored liqueur, if desired**

Heat oven to 400°. In 1-quart saucepan, heat water and butter to rolling boil. Stir in flour. Stir vigorously over low heat until mixture forms a ball, about 1 minute. Remove from heat. Beat in eggs, all at one time, until smooth. Drop dough by scant ¼ cupfuls 3 inches apart onto ungreased baking sheet (makes 6 puffs). Bake until puffed and golden, about 35 minutes. Cool.

Cut off tops of 2 cream puffs. Pull out any filaments of soft dough. Fill puffs with ice cream. Mix chocolate syrup and liqueur; drizzle on cream puffs. *2 puffs— and 4 more for other times*.

Note: Store the extra puffs unfilled and serve the following day or wrap in aluminum foil, label and freeze. To serve, fill with sweetened whipped cream, ice cream or pudding.

**Classic Beef Stroganoff
Poppy Seed Noodles
Cherry Tomato-Brussels Sprouts Salad
Hot Crusty Rolls
Peaches Flambé**

CLASSIC BEEF STROGANOFF

½ to ¾ **pound beef sirloin or round steak, about
½ inch thick**
2 **tablespoons butter or margarine**
¼ **pound mushrooms, sliced, or 1 can (4½ ounces)
sliced mushrooms, drained**
1 **small onion, finely chopped (about ¼ cup)**
½ **cup water**
1 **beef bouillon cube**
1 **tablespoon catsup**
1 **small clove garlic, finely chopped, or ⅛ teaspoon
instant minced garlic**
½ **teaspoon salt
Poppy Seed Noodles (at right)**
¼ **cup water**
1 **tablespoon flour**
½ **cup dairy sour cream**

Cut meat into strips, 1½ x ½ inch. Melt butter in 8-inch
skillet; cook and stir mushrooms and onion until onion
is tender. Remove vegetables from skillet.

In same skillet, brown meat over medium heat. Stir
in ½ cup water, the bouillon cube, catsup, garlic and
salt. Reduce heat; cover and simmer 15 minutes (45

minutes if using round steak; if necessary, add small amount of water). While meat simmers, prepare Poppy Seed Noodles.

Mix ¼ cup water and the flour; stir into meat mixture. Add mushrooms and onion. Heat to boiling, stirring constantly. Boil and stir 1 minute. Stir in sour cream and heat through. Serve on the noodles. *2 servings.*

POPPY SEED NOODLES

Cook 4 ounces noodles (about 1½ cups) in 1 quart boiling salted water (2 teaspoons salt) until tender, about 7 minutes. Drain noodles and return to saucepan. Add 1 tablespoon butter or margarine and 1 teaspoon poppy seed and toss.

CHERRY TOMATO-BRUSSELS SPROUTS SALAD

   ½ **package (10-ounce size) frozen Brussels sprouts***
   ¼ **cup oil-and-vinegar dressing or Italian dressing**
   1 **cup cherry tomatoes**
   2 **lettuce cups**

Cook Brussels sprouts as directed except—use only half the amounts of water and salt called for on package. Drain. Pour dressing on hot Brussels sprouts. Cover and refrigerate at least 3 hours.

Cut tomatoes into halves; add to Brussels sprouts and toss. Serve in lettuce cups. *2 servings.*

* Leftover frozen Brussels sprouts? Serve later in the week as the vegetable at another meal. Especially good with ham, pork or turkey.

PEACHES FLAMBÉ

       Vanilla ice cream
   2   tablespoons apricot jam
   2   tablespoons sugar
   ¼   cup water
   ½   teaspoon lemon juice
   1   can (8¾ ounces) sliced peaches, drained
   2   tablespoons brandy

Scoop ice cream into balls; place in freezer while
preparing sauce. In small chafing dish or saucepan,
heat jam, sugar, water and lemon juice, stirring occasionally, until syrupy, about 5 minutes. Add peaches
and heat through. Heat brandy until warm; pour on
peaches and ignite immediately. Spoon peaches and
sauce on ice cream. *2 servings*.

INDEX

183